Finishing History Well

Preparing for the Leadership of Jesus

Paul Hughes

Book Two in the Finishing Well Series

PRESS

The Finishing Well Series by Paul Hughes.
Finishing Life Well is focused on Christian Discipleship.
Finishing History Well is focused on Christian Eschatology.

Coming in 2013. . .
Will Cities Finish Well? is focused on the regional transformation Mission of the Church.

www.xulonpress.com
www.kingdomforerunners.com

For Lucy

Contents

The Finishing Well Series

A Simple Request

I never intended to write a book. In April of 2007 I started writing and couldn't stop. It took five years, but what I thought would be one book, became two!

These books grew out of a simple request of Jesus in late February of 2006. I was sitting on a stump in some woods by a stream in Kentucky. I was fasting and praying at the time, when I heard Him whisper in my heart, "Ask Me for anything." It was one of those moments when you feel your whole life could change depending on what happened next. After searching my heart for my greatest desire, I made a simple request.

"I want to finish well."

Life is Short, Eternity Isn't

At fifty-four, I can attest that life is fragile and short. Five months after my simple request, I played several pretty decent full court basketball games in a gym without air conditioning against a bunch of young adults. I crossed up one of my sons at mid-court with a fancy dribble and later hit the last shot to win the game for our team. At least that is how I remember it!

The next day, I had a stroke and could have died. The stroke happened in a country with a "stan" at the end of its name and there was no one qualified who could read an image from the one CT scanner within its borders. It didn't look good for me. But I am still here.

Eternity is a heartbeat away. We all live at a time when biblical and historical conditions suggest our generation is moving quickly toward some kind of historic climax. If Jesus doesn't return, we, at the very least, will experience massive global shifts in the coming decades. How should we live? How do we separate what is precious and eternal from what is profane and fleeting?

I want my life and yours to finish well. How we finish our lives is about the heart choices we are making now. Growing in intimacy and obedience with Jesus in grace filled, Spirit empowered, truth centered community is how God shapes us for an eternal future of glorious partnership with Him. We are all hopelessly flawed, but because of God's great love, we can all receive strength for authentic greatness in this life and beyond.

God made each of us for greatness, because He made each of us in His own image. He put us in this world to change it according to His desires expressed through us collectively. That means we must live in constant prayerful conversation to know His heart and operate as His partner in the earth. That is what the Holy Spirit does. He constantly gives us the mind of Jesus! God wants a people who live in the same courageous Holy Spirit as His Son.

Finishing Life Well is about how we can participate now in the Kingdom Jesus is bringing in fullness in the future.

Finishing History Well explores the main biblical views of the End-Times to prepare our generation for what lies ahead.

Will Cities Finishing Well? is about the transformation of cities and regions by the corporate prayers and obedience of the unified Church.

Fixing our eyes

During any historical transition, God's righteousness and Man's sinfulness mature together. The light gets brighter against a darkening sky. Fixing our eyes on Jesus, the leader of the future, will get us through the night. By anyone's standard, the life of Jesus of Nazareth stands alone in history. No one is more controversial, or compelling. No one is more loved, or hated. If He isn't the God-Man, there is no close second. All my chips are on Him.

Following Jesus leadership involves creative, redemptive suffering for Him and the values of His Kingdom, but all who give themselves to Jesus inherit a joyful future that cannot be compared.

"Therefore we do not lose heart. Though outwardly we are wasting away, yet inwardly we are being renewed day by day. For our light and momentary troubles are achieving for us an eternal glory that far outweighs them all. So we fix our eyes not on what is seen, but on what is unseen, since what is seen is temporary, but what is unseen is eternal." 2 Corinthians 4:16-18

Let us live well, love well, finish well. . . and begin again well, under the leadership of our dearest Friend!

Acknowledgments

The Gift of Blurriness

Let me be honest about the voice of my writing in the *Finishing Well Series*. Sometimes I write in a style that appeals to my 25, 22, and 15 year old sons and their friends who hang out at our house. At other times, I write out of the college campus ministry voice in my head which values robust biblical thinking. After thirty years of ministry among college students I have come by that voice honestly. I have wrestled with which audience I am writing to; "Cool dad or serious thinker,. . . cool dad or serious thinker . . . cool dad. . ."

God made me "blurry." That is the word my brother-in-law used after reading a draft of this book . . . and he is a Bible college president! He said I have the "gift of blurriness." Is blurriness a *gift*?! So, after trying many times to isolate one audience in my head by using one style of writing. . . I gave up. Seriously. Some chapters are personal and experiential and others are academic and theological. Welcome to my blurry world!

Life is Blurry, but God is Good

Life has a way of moving in and out of focus. Not everything makes sense for more than ten minutes. We all need to find our little life story in the plot of a really big story. Without a bigger story our lives get stuck. For me that big story is the drama of human history and divine romance found in the 66 Books of the Bible.

The grand storyline of the Bible shows we are all on a common journey through time that is really going somewhere. Life and history have a point. Why? Because God is writing the story and He is good!

Therefore, I can look back through the lens of the writers of the 66 Books and make sense out of the blurry legacy of my ancestors. The Bible helps me make sense out of my heart's journey through the blurriness of my generation. Gazing on God, and His storyline for history, anchors me to a hope for the future and for eternity.

A Blurry History

As a Hughes, I come from Scotch-Irish-Welsh pioneers who hacked out a mountain home around 1800 in the Cherokee country of Western North Carolina. My ancestors panned for gold during the rush in North Georgia in the 1830's and helped found towns and churches in Alabama while holding slaves in the 1840's and 50's. They fought for the Confederacy in the Civil War in the 1860's and then stood on the side of racial justice with Dr. Martin Luther King, Jr. in the 1950's. Go figure.

I am the product of a Methodist preacher's home with a strong social justice conscience who got radically born again at age 19. I was powerfully shaped by InterVarsity Christian Fellowship at the University of North Carolina at Chapel Hill. I know what it is like to lead a college Bible study with two dozen students crammed into my dorm room and share the love of Jesus with my drunken Sigma Nu frat brothers and party girls later the same night. As a business major, I took my degree and had a blast in the marketplace world for two years before joining IVCF's full-time campus ministry staff for more than twenty-five incredibly fruitful years. I had LOVED the business world. It felt strange for me to be called a minister.

I am a denominational mutt. Lucy and I have been a part of United Methodist, Presbyterian (PCA), African-American Missionary Baptist, Southern Baptist, and independent charismatic fellowships. I value the drama and beauty of liturgical worship in Catholic, Orthodox, and Anglican traditions. I can speak as an intellectual and also speak in tongues and fall on the floor as a Pentecostal.

I love Jews, Muslims, Hindus, Pagans, and Secular Humanists enough to listen to them, honestly disagree, and try to introduce them to the Jesus I know. I love the smells and ordered chaos of an Uzbekistan Bazaar and I can't wait to get back to Wal-Mart. I can comfortably walk alone across a Black College campus late at night in the "bad part" of town and then sleep in my suburban neighborhood with a pool in our back yard.

I love people. I seek to connect with strangers on their terms in their world, and yet I am haunted by the clear message of the Bible that while we all share the same present, we will not all share the same eternity. A day of judgment is coming and I must warn people I know in a way they understand.

So, I *am* blurry. Hopelessly blurry. Maybe it is because I am wet clay on the Master Potter's wheel just like you. Spinning around, lumps and all, taking shape under the loving pressure of His firm, but gentle hands. Maybe we are *all* blurry, because none of us sees God fully. None of us sees the whole picture of history. None of us can fit every piece of the Bible together.

I have only one non-negotiable in my life. Jesus. He has the last word over all of me. Every thought. Every emotion. Every action. Every relationship. Every decision. He is the one still point in my blurry world.

Many to Thank

There are many who have known Jesus with me whose voices come out in my writing. Some are the voices of lives lived well in the past who still speak in my heart. Dead theologians like Francis Schaeffer and George E. Ladd have helped me write this book. I hope their influences will be word ramps for you toward a greater understanding of "The God Who Is There".

Dr. Jack Arnold was my pastor for eleven years at Covenant Presbyterian Church (PCA) in Winter Park, Florida. Jack and his wife Carol came to faith in Jesus in the home of Bill and Vonette Bright during the early days of Campus Crusade for Christ at UCLA.

A classmate of famous author Hal Lindsey, Jack earned a doctorate from Dallas Theological Seminary while winning the top award for Systematic Theology. Over the years, Jack transitioned from Dispensational Theology to Grace Covenant Theology and taught as an adjunct professor at Reformed Theological Seminary in Orlando. His death while preaching in 2005 made national news. Cleartheology.com digitizes 60 of Jack's teaching series and 1200 of his sermons and lessons.

Another of those dead theologians is my Dad, Miles Preston Hughes, Jr. who graduated to Heaven when I was fifteen years old. His 1946 Duke Divinity School thesis, *A Study in the Meaning of Christian Hope in the Epistles of Paul* is remarkable. It is one of those intergenerational batons that I am carrying as I pass it on to the generation coming up behind me.

One of those fast approaching next generation theologians is my oldest son, Gabriel. In many ways I am already following him. As a graduate of Southeastern Bible College and current seminarian at Beeson Divinity School he often pointed me to excellent sources used in these pages. During 2010, Gabriel and several other twenty-something friends planted Hope Culture Church in Birmingham where our whole family worships. I have the privilege of being a senior elder at Hope Culture, but the genius of this amazing expression of church lies in the God of Abraham, Isaac, and Jacob; the God who reveals Himself throughout all generations and desires that all worship Him from an authentic heart.

Our whole family is impacted by the International House of Prayer in Kansas City founded by Mike Bickle. The 24/7 prayer community that began in September of 1999 under Mike's leadership is a sign and wonder in our world today. Mike's associate director is Allen Hood, the President of the IHOP University. Allen is the one who commended my blurriness! He believes my writing weaves biblical concepts into a clearer big picture. You be the judge. Allen is also my brother-in-law and close friend.

National prayer leader and founder of The Call prayer movement, Lou Engle, has also been a major voice in my life. On November 3, 2003 Lou prayed a blessing over me in a dirty downtown warehouse. "God, give this man the desires of his heart for a house of prayer in Birmingham." I am still on that journey, Lou!

Allen Hood, Gary Greene, Jenny Keck, Ed Hackett and I married into the amazing Jack and Beth Downey family and have never been the same! "Poppa D" and "Momma D" sired the culture of the Kingdom into their five kids in a way that is revolutionizing the world. All of their children, their spouses, grandkids, grandkid spouses, and great grandkids, not only love each as best friends, but we all together are best friends with Jesus. In an era when marriage and family is in shambles, we experience a Christ-centered loyalty that covers our many weaknesses as we press on toward knowing the Lord. I have no way of deciphering the untold number of ideas in this book that are the product of family discussions and prayer times.

Though few realize it, the influence of the Eastern North Carolina gentility of my Mom, Helen Prince Hughes Rice, is in my every pore. She still embodies the best of Southern graces where under the broad shady oaks of Dunn, North Carolina she grew up with playmates who knew a simpler world, genuinely more moral than the one today. More than once she tempered my gloomy soap box family room sermons with hope for a better world in the Jesus she knew. I am a better man for it.

It is my Mom's Prince/Hood family tree that I have to thank for the early Pentecostal influences. In 1906 a Holiness preacher named G. B. Cashwell returned to his native Dunn from the famous Azusa Street Revival in Los Angeles. His own January 1907 three week revival in a tobacco warehouse earned him the title "Apostle of Pentecostalism to the South." Cashwell would influence the founders of around a dozen denominations, including the Assemblies of God and the Church of God (Cleveland, TN). His legacy would also influence my Mom's grandparents, Momma and Poppa Hood.

Poppa Hood's booming prayers could be heard outside of the stately Divine Street Methodist Episcopal Church South where he led the Methodist Men. While remaining faithful to Methodism, Momma Hood would often attend the Pentecostal Holiness Church around the corner from Divine Street Methodist. My mother fondly remembers when Poppa and Momma Hood would take her as a girl.

to fiery Pentecostal Holy Ghost tent revivals. I cherish that some of the "sawdust trail" sticks to the feet of my ancestors.

I am a huge product of the culture of InterVarsity Christian Fellowship. Many of the stellar people I have known in ministry have been a part of the IVCF family. There are far too many former students and ministry colleagues for me to acknowledge here, but I do want to single out Bruce Alwood. Bruce, you patiently supervised me through the years of transition from campus work to the founding of a whole new ministry. This writing project began during my nine month ministry sabbatical of 2007. How grateful I am for InterVarsity's pastoral culture which helps people exiting employment to transition well. Bruce, you did it for me, man!

I am grateful to Pastor Bart Brookins and the faith family at Fullness Christian Fellowship who loved my family well while books were written, Kingdom Forerunners was launched, and Hope Culture Church was birthed. It is churches like Fullness that are helping Birmingham become the city of Jesus' dreams.

The Birmingham Prayer Furnace is indebted to other local churches, like Metro Church of God while under Mark Schrade, and Living Church Ministries under Bishop Demetrics and Pauline Roscoe. I am also grateful for ministries with city-wide vision like The Lovelady Center under Brenda Spahn, Joshua Generation under Jody Trautwein, Love Well Ministries under Lestley Drake, the Metro Birmingham Evangelical Ministers Association under Jack Eyer, prayer leadership partners like Kevin Moore with Mission Birmingham, Mark Miller with the Greater Birmingham Mayor's Prayer Breakfast, and Birmingham Police Chief A.C. Roper with Prayer Force United.

At the state level, I am grateful for the inspirational leadership of Kyle Searcy, Director of the Alabama Alliance of Reformation and Pastor of Fresh Anointing House of Worship in Montgomery. It is an honor for Lucy and me to be ordained under his pastoral authority. Brother, Kyle, because of men of God like you, incredible things are ahead for the Body of Christ in Alabama!

I am grateful for those I share the long journey with for restoring honor to Native Americans; Dale Cathey with Servants of Christ, Tom Dooley of Pathclearers, Cherokee leader Randy Woodley,

Muscogee Creek minister Melba Checote Eads, Yuchi leader Negiel Bigpond, and Inuit leader Suuquina. Justice is coming.

Internationally, the Birmingham Prayer Furnace and the Campus Prayer Networks are deeply influenced by the values of our friends Pete Grieg, David Blackwell, Nathan and Marisa Chud, Ryan and Allison Riggs, and others with the 24/7 Prayer and Boiler Room communities. Thanks blokes!

To the Kingdom Forerunners board; wow. What a journey God has us on! Al and Danielle, John and Cindy, Brett and Kenzie, Lucy and I can't imagine dreaming these impossible dreams for God's Kingdom to come on earth through 24/7 prayer, justice, and mission with anyone else! You guys believe in the vision when no one else has a clue. Your voices in my life keep me believing, too.

Thanks to Kingdom Forerunners staff and former staff Gabriel Hughes, Ike Ubasineke, Pierre Blackman, Jared Fonseca, Erica Jackson, Natalie Farber, Tim and Ericka Frye, Matt Makar, Adrienne Scott, Jeff Davis, Kelly Curtler, Sherei Jackson, Emily Day, Brent McGough, Carly Downey, Clayton Mullins, Jana Laher, Taylor Webb, Matt and Holly Hobson, and the many volunteer singers, musicians, and intercessors filling the bowls of prayer in Heaven from out of the Birmingham Prayer Furnace! Nothing happens without prayer! May these books find their way into your hands and hearts to better fashion prayers of faith that prepare us, our families, our city, our region, and this global generation for the leadership of Jesus.

Finally, no one, other than Jesus, deserves more gratitude or has more claim of influence on me than my wife, Lucy. Honey, it is your life that has helped me to best know the one Voice that matters most. I have done the writing, but you have done the loving that made it possible. You hear the urgency of our moment in history when others do not. Many things are blurry around us, but Sweetheart, with one certain voice we stand as a man and woman together with our three amazing sons (and the women who love them) to declare to all who are listening. . . Jesus is coming. People get ready.

Introduction

*"Be ready, for the Son of Man is coming at an hour
you do not expect."*
(Matthew 24:44)

Pressing Questions

When loved ones know that a parting is near, one of the pressing questions is, "When will we see each other again?"

In Matthew chapter 24, Jesus had an important conversation with his closest friends around that very question. One of the questions of this book is much the same as theirs. "What kind of world will exist when Jesus returns and will *we* be alive when it happens?" That question sells a lot of books. Some are scary and full of sensationalism. Some are highly academic and inaccessible to most readers. Some are plain weird. Some are all of the above.

I believe there are straight-forward biblical and historical reasons to prepare for Jesus to physically lead the planet soon. I want to make that case in a way that a serious young adult can understand. Jesus is coming and we are *so* not ready.

Setting the Tone

This book is about understanding biblical End Time views and contrasting philosophies. Because the Kingdom of God is both a present *AND* a coming Kingdom, it is a challenging and complex topic on a cognitive level. There is blurriness because we live in overlapping Ages. Jesus said the Kingdom of God has come and the Kingdom of God is coming. So we embrace divine tension while trusting in God's goodness. There is no confusion in God's love. We can cooperate confidently with His Spirit without having the clarity of full comprehension. God has us. We will gain more clarity as God's plan in history matures.

The subject of finishing history well is serious stuff. I don't want to minimize the depth of the temporary perils and eternal consequences we all face. I believe in a real Heaven and real Hell. I believe in a real Messiah and a real Devil. But above all else, I believe that God our Father is the most glad, beautiful, merciful, loving, powerful, and creative being of all. He does all things for His greatest pleasure and our greatest good. Loving us and receiving our love really impacts Him. So my understanding of God is colored by the idea that He is doing *everything*, short of violating our free will, to help us all finish well and wind up in His embrace. The fact that He has not destroyed us already, in spite of our constant rejection of His leadership, is a sign of His great love and patience.

Paul was a follower of Jesus who suffered greatly for spreading the news of Jesus' global leadership to the first century world. In spite of all his trials he trumpeted, "Rejoice in the Lord always! Again I say rejoice!" In our confusing world filled with the reality of human tragedy, we all need to understand that God's shakings are, in fact, merciful wake-up calls. Personal and global crises are best understood in the light of an eternity led by a good, good Father. A God who sends His own Son to die in our place deserves to be taken seriously. The Son who took the bullet meant for us deserves to be our leader. A better world is coming and our Dad really wants *you* to be there.

Until that world comes, it is safe to say that everyone on the planet will experience tension. On a given day, you and I might be tempted to exchange our set of problems. But we all have problems and we all experience anxiety. Whether you believe that the 66

Books of the Bible can be trusted or not doesn't mean you may not still be bothered by what it says about you and your life. . . or *us* and *our* future. If you *are* bothered or curious enough to read this book, good! Keep reading, you may just get a few answers or better questions than the ones you have now. You may have some tension relieved, but not all.

Jesus *creates* a divine tension when He tells His friends that no one but His Father in Heaven knows exactly when His adored Son will return to the Earth. Was keeping the exact timing of Jesus' physical return a mystery intended by our Good Father to be an incentive for His kids to chill out? Not hardly! The goal of the intrigue was to heighten the motivation and alertness of all who would come to discover Jesus and want to follow Him across the centuries.

Is this book a sweeping set of elaborate End Time scenarios implying you should sell your retirement funds and move into a cave? No. Do we need to discern our time wisely in order to live well and be prepared for Jesus' leadership over the world soon? Yes. At least if you take the Bible seriously.

The Beginning of Birth Pangs

The historical and spiritual conditions that Jesus said would ripen during the generations before His return are unfolding before our eyes. During the conversation on the Mount of Olives overlooking the Temple Mount in Jerusalem, Jesus' friends asked Him, "What will be the sign of your coming and of the end of the age?" Jesus answered:

Watch out that no one deceives you. For many will come in my name, claiming, 'I am the Christ, and will deceive many. You will hear of wars and rumors of wars, but see to it that you are not alarmed. Such things must happen, but the end is still to come. Nation will rise against nation, and kingdom against kingdom. There will be famines and earthquakes in various places. All these are the beginning of birth pains. (Matthew 24:3-8)

Since false religious movements, political conflicts, natural and manmade disasters are general signs that describe the last twenty centuries many Christians wonder why our generation is any different?

Part of the answer to that question has to do with how significantly one views the creation of the political State of Israel in 1948. Some Christian leaders across the world, because of their Church tradition, national politics, or training in how to interpret the Bible, see no particular significance to the reappearance of a modern Israeli state in the Middle East.

Some of Jesus' predictions concerning Israel, particularly the Roman destruction of the Jewish Second Temple, were literally fulfilled during events of the first century AD. But it is my view that other parts of Jesus' predictions for ethnic Israel remain ahead of us. Consider the increasing presence of ethnic Jews living in the Middle East as a precondition of His return.

I write this book using an interpretive grid of future events that theologians call the Historic Premillennial view. This view holds that Gentiles (or non-Jews) are incorporated by their trust in Jesus into the same covenant family of Abraham. Jesus created One New Man out of Jews and Gentiles on the cross. This new creation is the "Church" and, as the inheritors of the covenant promises given to Old Testament saints like Abraham and King David, the Church is "spiritual Israel". At the same time, cultural and biological Jews (the ethnic descendents of Abraham) have been preserved by God through history for a future acceptance of the leadership of Jesus as He returns. At that time Jesus will establish Jerusalem as the center of His leadership over the world for a thousand years, fulfilling God's promises to Israel for a full restoration during a Global Messianic Kingdom.

Preconditions of the Return of Jesus

Christians will differ on the particular events and their sequence around the return of Jesus, but two major preconditions are nearing fulfillment our generation.

Condition 1 – *Jesus' Great Commission in Matthew 28:18 and Matthew 14:24 to make citizen-priests of His Kingdom from every culture on earth is nearing completion.*

As Jesus was leaving the Earth to take up temporary residence in Heaven, He commissioned His followers to take the message and lifestyle of His Kingdom to every culture on the globe.

Then Jesus came to them and said, "All authority in heaven and on earth has been given to me. Therefore go and make disciples of all nations, baptizing them in the name of the Father and of the Son and of the Holy Spirit, and teaching them to obey everything I have commanded you. And surely I am with you always, to the very end of the age. (Matthew 28:18-20)

And this Gospel of the Kingdom will be preached in the whole world as a testimony to all nations, and then the end will come. (Matthew 24:14)

For the first time in history it is entirely possible that this mandate from Jesus will be finished in our lifetime. Mark Anderson and Paul Eshleman lead an initiative with the Call2All organization which helps direct evangelism to the remaining Unengaged, Unreached People Groups. In 2007, there were 639 UUPG's. By 2010, mission work had already begun in 469 of them!

To be sure, the criteria used to measure the growth and durability of Christian communities is not an exact science in an ever changing social and spiritual environment, but the overall trend is clear. Unprecedented numbers of people and cultures outside of the Western World *are* receiving the message of Jesus.

Are there set-backs? Yes. Many of the "gospels" are weak, containing corrupt ideas that don't produce strong lovers of Jesus. For example, Muslims are coming to Jesus in numbers unlike anything ever seen in history; but many of these converts are suffocated by the overwhelming oppression of their Islamic cultures, do not reproduce their faith, or eventually return to Islam. Western societies, where the message of the 66 Books of the Bible have been preached for generations, are mired in dead religious tradition, divorce, immorality, selfish ambition, greed, pride, abortion, racism, political idolatry, and ignorance of the real Jesus or His Kingdom's value system.

In spite of all human failure and demonic opposition over thousands of years, the influence of God's Kingdom *is* steadily advancing across the global community. The message of Jesus the Messiah preached by those who love Him *is* God's unstoppable power at work to resuscitate dead human hearts and minds. The victory of God's Kingdom is not in doubt. The real question is how many in our world will say "Yes!" to the authority of God's King before He comes in power.

Condition 2 – *The creation of a national homeland for Jews in 1948 in the land of ancient Israel and the subsequent re-gathering of global Jewry sets the stage for end time Bible prophecy to be fulfilled.*

"O Jerusalem, Jerusalem, you who kill the prophets and stone those sent to you, how often I have longed to gather your children together, as a hen gathers her chicks under her wings, but you were not willing. Look, your house is left to you desolate. For I tell you, you will not see me again until you say, 'Blessed is he who comes in the name of the Lord.'" (Matthew 23:37-39)

In the above passage, Jesus was speaking to the Jewish leaders of Jerusalem who rejected His leadership over His Father's House and the nation. They are long gone. Matthew 23:39 predicts there will be a future generation of Jewish elders who will *welcome* His leadership when Jerusalem is established as God's capital at Jesus' return.

Any world leader, regardless of personal or national politics, has to deal with the explosive potential of Jerusalem and its major political players. But going on practically unnoticed in Israel-Palestine is a group that is not Muslim or Christian Arab, not Orthodox or secular Jew, and not foreign political and business resident. It is the Israeli Jewish follower of Jesus.

I don't want to exaggerate the magnitude of the current Messianic Jewish movement in Israel. Some would claim that the estimated 15,000 Israeli Jewish followers of Jesus are not a statistically significant number. Others will point out that they are often poor, divided, and have virtually no political muscle. In some ways, that describes the Jews who followed Jesus in Israel during the days of the New Testament.

Is it inevitable that their number and impact will grow? Humanly speaking, no. Is it a phenomenon that such a community is alive and growing in Israel again after 1900 years? I believe it is. In the generation of the Lord's return, I believe the trickle of ethnic Jews becoming followers of Jesus in Israel and around the world will turn into a flood. As Jesus predicted in Matthew 23:39, changing conditions on the Earth will lead the Jewish leaders of Jerusalem to welcome Him as their Messiah when He returns.

Depending on one's interpretation of the Bible there are other preconditions yet to come. The rise of an "Anti-Christ" global leader, the possibility of a Third Jewish Temple on the Temple Mount in Jerusalem, a great falling away of those who call themselves Christians, a period of great trouble for the whole world and the Church, and a great harvest of many who accept the leadership of Jesus.

The preceding two preconditions are observable, but these next two have yet to appear. I want to place these next preconditions on the global watch list.

Condition 3 – *A third rebuilt Jewish Temple may be necessary in order to fulfill prophecies of what a future Anti-Christ leader will do in Daniel 9:27 and Matthew 24:15; and what two amazing preachers will do in Revelation 11.*

During the 6th century BC, the Old Testament prophet Daniel is given insight from the angel Gabriel, concerning future events:

The people of the ruler who will come will destroy the city and the sanctuary. The end will come like a flood: War will continue until the end, and desolations have been decreed. He* will confirm a covenant with many for one 'seven.' In the middle of the 'seven' he will put an end to sacrifice and offering. And on a wing of the temple he will set up an abomination that causes desolation, until the end that is decreed is poured out on him. (Daniel 9:26-27) *perhaps the Anti-Christ

In Matthew 24:15, Jesus references the above passage:

So when you see standing in the holy place (the temple) 'the abomination that causes desolation,' spoken of through the prophet Daniel—let the reader understand—then let those who are in Judea flee to the mountains.

Matthew Chapter 24 begins with Jesus making a disturbing prediction concerning the destruction of the Second Temple that stood in Jerusalem at that time. As the center of worship, the Temple represented Israel's national purpose and identity as the covenant people of God. That troubling statement is what caused the disciples to ask the pressing question, "When will this happen?"

Jesus left the temple and was walking away when his disciples came up to him to call his attention to its buildings. "Do you see all these things?" he asked. "I tell you the truth, not one stone here will be left on another; every one will be thrown down."

As Jesus was sitting on the Mount of Olives, the disciples came to him privately. "Tell us," they said, "when will this happen, and what will be the sign of your coming and of the end of the age?"

The Temple was destroyed by the Romans in 70 AD. Jewish followers of Jesus did flee Judea for the mountains to escape the Roman siege. According to the Jewish historian, Josephus, there were abominable acts committed by Roman commanders before the Temple was burned and dismantled, fitting Daniel's and Jesus' prophecies. "Preterism" is the term for the case that Jesus' predictions in Matthew 24 were *all* fulfilled in the first century.

But other parts of Matthew 24 seem to be pointing beyond 70 AD to a future and global event in which Jesus comes visibly to all.

For as lightning that comes from the east is visible even in the west, so will be the coming of the Son of Man. At that time the sign of the Son of Man will appear in the sky, and all the nations of the earth will mourn. They will see the Son of Man coming on the clouds of the sky, with power and great glory. And he will send his angels with a loud trumpet call, and they will gather his elect from the four winds, from one end of the heavens to the other. (Matthew 24:27, 30-31)

According to the strongest and earliest church traditions, the apostle John wrote the Revelation around 95 AD, twenty plus years after the Second Jewish Temple was destroyed. Daniel had a vision of a future temple while none existed as he wrote. Likewise, John may be seeing a future temple in Jerusalem where two powerful figures preach the coming of Jesus during a three and a half year period under a newly revealed Anti-Christ.

I was given a reed like a measuring rod and was told, "Go and measure the temple of God and the altar, and count the worshipers there. But exclude the outer court; do not measure it, because it has been given to the Gentiles. They will trample on the holy city for 42 months. And I will give power to my two witnesses, and they will prophesy for 1,260 days, clothed in sackcloth. Now when they have finished their testimony, the beast that comes up from the Abyss will attack them, and overpower and kill them. Their bodies will lie in the street of the great city, which is figuratively called Sodom and Egypt, where also their Lord was crucified." (Revelation 11: 1-3, 7-8)

Most scholars interpret the Beast in Revelation as the Roman Empire. Rome was persecuting the churches in the Province of Asia to whom John was writing. The Roman cult of emperor worship, with its immoral pagan temple rituals was making war on the Church. John wrote to a specific audience at a specific time using language that made perfect sense to the Churches in their political and cultural context.

Two thousand years have passed. Jesus has not physically returned to Jerusalem. The Roman Empire no longer exists. How do we interpret John's revelation to our world today? *Should we* interpret John's vision to today?

The visions of temples in Daniel's 6th century BC and in John's late first century AD both have past and, I believe, future relevance.

xxix

Theologian George Ladd of the mid 20ᵗʰ century championed the "now and not yet" view of God's Kingdom and the prophetic writings of the Bible that are linked to it. If one accepts that there are past and future aspects to Daniel and John's temple visions, then, in principle, one needs to be open to a rebuilt Third Jewish Temple being defiled by some type of future Anti-Christ Empire.

If built, a Third Temple in Jerusalem will not house the presence of God. The Holy Spirit now dwells in the hearts of true followers of Jesus. The Body of Christ as people, not a building, is the dwelling place of God in the Earth today. Since a Third Temple is politically implausible and spiritually unnecessary, the reasons it would reappear would be to fulfill prophecy and to redeem the hearts of Jews.

So. . . are events connected to the tiny real estate of the Temple Mount part of God's preparation of the global community toward a final climax? This question is at the center of much theological debate in the global Church today.

It is hard for any citizen of our planet; Christian, Jew, Muslim, or anyone else, to deny that the same ground where God provided a ram in the bush as a substitute for Abraham's son Isaac millennia ago is not the political epicenter of our human family today. The Muslim Dome of the Rock probably stands over the very site where bulls, goats, and sheep were sacrificed in the Jewish Temple up until the time of Jesus. That small contested hill of Mount Zion represents the pin of the global hand grenade we all live on.

After the destruction of Jerusalem and the Second Jewish Temple by the Romans in 70 AD and the scattering of the Jewish nation when the Roman army crushed the Bar Kochba Jewish revolt in 135 AD, the idea of a third Jewish Temple being built seemed impossible for centuries. But when the Temple Mount in Jerusalem was restored to national Israel after a dramatic conflict with neighboring Arab countries in 1967 the scenario became more plausible.

Condition 4 – *A time of Great Tribulation comes during which Jews and followers of Jesus are specifically targeted as enemies of a global state (or network of states) led by an Anti-Christ leader. The three and half years before Jesus splits the skies will be the hard labor required to birth a golden Messianic Age.*

In Matthew 24:21-22, Jesus said:

For then there will be great distress, unequaled from the beginning of the world until now—and never to be equaled again. If those days had not been cut short, no one would survive, but for the sake of the elect those days will be shortened.

If Jesus were referring entirely to the horrible events that surrounded the Roman destruction of Jerusalem in 70 AD, then it is difficult with our 21st century hindsight to reconcile how the great distress being described then was not surpassed by the Nazi holocaust of six million Jews during World War II. The sobering conclusion is that if the Jewish holocaust was also not the great distress just before the return of Jesus, there remains an *even greater* distress ahead for Jews and Christians.

The great distress is commonly called the Great Tribulation. In a Premillennial view, the Great Tribulation begins with the events of Matthew 24:15 which describe the defilement of the Jewish Temple by a newly revealed Anti-Christ.

So when you see standing in the holy place (the temple) 'the abomination that causes desolation,' spoken of through the prophet Daniel—let the reader understand—then let those who are in Judea flee to the mountains.

Revelation 13:5-8 gives more information about the Anti-Christ, referred to as the Beast. We see that his rule will be three and a half years and it involves persecution of the Church while receiving the worship due to Jesus to himself:

The beast was given a mouth to utter proud words and blasphemies and to exercise his authority for forty-two months. He opened his mouth to blaspheme God, and to slander his name and his dwelling place and those who live in heaven. He was given power to make war against the saints and to conquer them. And he was given authority over every tribe, people, language and nation. All inhabitants of the earth will worship the beast— all whose names have not been written in the book of life belonging to the Lamb that was slain from the creation of the world.

In Matthew 24, Jesus indicated that His future followers, particularly the generation of His return, would face great trials *because of Him.* Our faithfulness to Jesus in the midst of pressure reflects the overall tension of Kingdoms in conflict and offers the certainty of future restoration under the leadership of Jesus which our world will need.

Then you will be handed over to be persecuted and put to death, and you will be hated by all nations because of me. At that time many will turn away from the faith and will betray and hate each other, and many false prophets will appear and deceive many people. Because of the increase of wickedness, the love of most will grow cold, but he who stands firm to the end will be saved. (Matthew 24:9-13)

Matthew 24:29-31 reveals what follows the Great Tribulation:

Immediately after the distress of those days the sun will be darkened, and the moon will not give its light; the stars will fall from the sky, and the heavenly bodies will be shaken At that time the sign of the Son of Man will appear in the sky, and all the nations of the earth will mourn. They will see the Son of Man coming on the clouds of the sky, with power and great glory. And he will send his angels with a loud trumpet call, and they will gather his elect from the four winds, from one end of the heavens to the other.

Jesus tells his followers that the Great Tribulation begins with the abomination of desolation in the Jewish Temple and ends with His return in power. Not all Premillennialists believe in a literal 1260 day or 3 ½ year Great Tribulation. For some the whole Church Age is the tribulation. The length of Jesus' earthly ministry from John's baptism to His Ascension to Heaven is roughly 3 ½ years. I anticipate there will be a literal 3 ½ year period of hard labor before the Jesus returns in the fullness of His Kingdom. Just as Jesus modeled in his public life how to press through all that the world, His own weak flesh, and the Devil had to throw at Him, I see the future global Church carrying our cross those final 3 ½ years. The last of the last days will be the hardest ground to cover, but there will be abundant grace for all who persevere.

In the literal interpretation, the Tribulation and Great Tribulation are not synonymous. The length of the entire Tribulation is seven years. The theory is that a world in crisis will give rise to the Anti- Christ leader, presumably a man with great personal charisma, spiritual power, and diplomatic influence. The Premillennial interpretation of Daniel 9:27 is this man will rescue the world from the brink of destruction through a world peace agreement involving Israel. This powerful leader will betray that peace treaty with Israel after three and a half years, ushering in the final three and a half years of Great Tribulation.

The Anti-Christ government will require the total allegiance, even worship, of all people. Followers of Jesus will have no choice but to resist this global religion. This will produce waves of martyrs unlike anything since the persecutions of Jesus-lovers under Roman Emperors Nero, Domitian, and Diocletian in the first Christian centuries. But our Savior will be NEAR! True followers of Jesus will be willing and confident to lay down their lives in love for others and in witness for Christ.

All of the Church Age since Jesus ascended to Heaven has seen tribulation. We live in Kingdoms that are in mortal conflict. Jesus promised, "In the world you will have tribulation, but be of good cheer, I have overcome the world!" So we ARE in the tribulation now. But don't be surprised if the greatest global trouble comes just before that great and terrible Day of the Lord's return.

I want my children and their friends to be filled with the knowledge of God and the fire of His Spirit's presence now and in those coming days. To prepare for the leadership of Jesus means to resist the leadership of the Anti-Jesus who comes before Him. That is why I have written this book. So you and I may finish history well together.

Finishing History Well

Preparing for the Leadership of Jesus

"My food," said Jesus, *"is to do the will of Him who sent Me and to finish His work."*
John 4:34

Chapter 1

Preparing for the Leadership of Jesus

"In the past God overlooked such ignorance,
but now He commands all people everywhere to repent.
For He has set a day when He will judge the world with justice by
the man He has appointed. He has given proof of this to all men by
raising Him from the dead."
(Acts 17:30-31)

Surfing History

There isn't much I like on TV these days, but I sometimes get hooked by the History Channel. One series depicted how the world will do just fine without us. And we ate it up.

Hello? What is so entertaining about a planet without people? That's just depressing. At least our nihilist friends at the History Channel have beautiful well edited special effects with which to serve up happy apocalyptic visions that sell us cars and deodorant. The cockroaches win! Isn't that sweet.

Real life and history is messy, but no thinking person can live happily for long without meaning. What if people were made with a destiny? What if the universe has a purpose? What if there is a God behind the drama of the human story after all? What if our collective human experience is heading toward an amazingly hopeful and vastly meaningful "future history"? Are we prepared to live in that kind of reality? These are important questions for every human being.

The meaning of history, God's activity in it, and where we, as a planet, are all going is a subject that puts us smack dab in the thick of the Bible. "Smack dab" is something we say here in Alabama. Like many sons of the South, I was given a good Bible name. My parents named me after Paul, the first century messenger of Jesus.

In Acts Chapter 17 my namesake was smack dab in the middle of Athens, Greece getting in trouble as usual for talking too much and too loud about the man named Jesus, a man that knocked him off his horse on a trip to Damascus. The intellectuals in town put Paul on their version of CNN. Listen to how Paul summarizes human history for them.

The God who made the world and everything in it is the Lord of Heaven and Earth and does not live in temples built by hands. And He is not served by human hands, as if He needed anything, because He Himself gives all men life and breath and everything else. From one man He made every nation of men, that they should inhabit the whole Earth; and He determined the times set for them and the exact places where they should live. God did this so that men would seek him and perhaps reach out for him and find him, though He is not far from each one of us. 'For in Him we live and move and have our being.' As some of your own poets have said, 'We are His offspring.'

Therefore since we are God's offspring, we should not think that the divine being is like gold or silver or stone—an image made by man's design and skill. In the past God overlooked such ignorance, but now He commands all people everywhere to repent. For He has set a day when He will judge the world with justice by the man He has appointed. He has given proof of this to all men by raising Him from the dead. (Acts 17:24-31)

Paul said a mouthful, so let's recap his sermon. God made everything and everybody. Check. He doesn't need us, but He sure seems interested in us. Check. God started human history on His terms and He intends to finish it on His terms. Check. He is the one who determines when, where, and why we are born. Check. He expects everybody on the planet to make searching out the truth of who He is and what He is like the top priority of their life. Check. He did not leave us clueless. There are signs pointing to God through the arts and stories of every culture. Check. Worshipping anything less than the real God is the stupidest idea ever. Check. All of history is leading to a Day of Judgment when Jesus, a dead guy who is alive again, will judge us all with perfect justice. Move over Judge Judy. Check.

Preaching the Future

When Paul preached the news about Jesus to the secular and religious audiences of his generation it was not a niche message applying only to a few. The message about Jesus is winner-take-all and the universe is what is on the table. It is very important to note that preaching Jesus has always meant preaching a particular way that history will climax for everyone. The Judge is coming and the Bible tells us exactly who He is.

Paul is more to the point when he writes to the gathering of believers in Thessalonica.

God is just: He will pay back trouble to those who trouble you and give relief to you who are troubled, and to us as well. This will happen when the Lord Jesus is revealed from Heaven in blazing fire with His powerful angels. He will punish those who do not know God and do not obey the Gospel of our Lord Jesus. They will be punished with everlasting destruction and shut out from the presence of the Lord and from the majesty of His power on the day He comes to be glorified with His holy people and to be marveled at among all those who have believed. (2 Thess. 1:7-10)

Paul was smart enough to preach the future in a way that different Greek audiences could handle its intensity. Do we want the Bible's clear message about the future Kingdom? Many people today really do not. If you do want to take the Bible's message of the coming Kingdom of God seriously, how much of the promise of the leadership of Jesus are you willing to live by now?

If you are a follower of Jesus, you need to be certain that the Bible is not history neutral. The 66 Books of the Bible we believe have authority over our lives are a product of history. They are written by real historical people. Its subject matter is very clear on the issue of what history is all about. All sixty-six books are variations of historical narrative, historical commentary, laws and regulations, real letters from real people to real places, and other historically relevant literary genres. We may be bored by the long lists of genealogies and censuses, but what does that say about the Bible? It is history. It is not fiction, or myth, or legend. Jesus talked about Jonah as a real person, not a fairy tale about a man who got swallowed by a fish.

The historical detail in the Bible reveals to us that God is not an "armchair quarterback." He is actively engaged with creation and human history. He knows the number of hairs on your head right now. He is not leaving the outcome of human history to chance, although the outcome of human history is left to choice; ours and God's.

Investing in the Future

The word used to describe the study of future events is "eschatology." This book isn't a highly technical treatment of the subject, but you do need to know where I stand in my understanding of what the Bible teaches about "End Times." What we think happens in the future determines how we invest our lives each day. If you invested in Google when it first hit the stock market, you are probably living in a big house right now. If you are investing your life in Jesus, you can't even imagine the kind of mansion that is waiting for you when He goes public. The meek inherit the Earth.

When Jesus comes, there will be a transfer of ownership and wealth involving the whole universe. It all belongs to Him. He is the rightful heir and He can't wait to share His wealth with His girlfriend, and soon to be Bride. But even though the good news about the coming Kingdom involves the biggest get-rich scheme ever, the value system of that Kingdom is completely opposite in many ways to this material world. Jesus preached a message in Matthew chapters five, six, and seven known as the Sermon on the Mount. It is the core values of His Kingdom. The first book in the *Finishing Well Series*, *Finishing Life Well*, develops those values. A Sermon on the Mount lifestyle is not for wimps or for those with selfish ambitions. To inherit this Kingdom you die to everything in this life. But it is so worth it!

If you could go back and invest in Google stock when it was first issued, you probably would. It is the same with the Kingdom of God. If everyone really knew how smart the offer was to die to self now to live as the betrothed Bride of Jesus, it would be a no-brainer. We receive this invisible Kingdom by receiving an invisible King. But the visible is just around the corner.

End Time Buffet

Concepts among Christians about how history will climax are diverse. Much of the breadth of opinion comes from *how* to read and interpret key chapters of the Bible found in books like Daniel, Ezekiel, and Revelation. The method one uses to interpret the Bible is called a "hermeneutic." The first appendix in the back of this book is an excellent summary of the two major ways biblical prophecy is interpreted. Depending on one's hermeneutic there are up to 150 chapters of the Bible that have an End Time theme. The climax of human history at the Day of the Lord is no small topic in the Bible. Rightly so. It is a wonderful and exciting subject. The future belongs to God and His people. Our wedding day is coming!

In the last of the 66 Books, Revelation 20:1-10 describes a one thousand year reign of Jesus with His saints ruling over the earth while Satan is imprisoned. Those verses are where the term "millennium" originates. This word comes from the Latin word "mille" for thousand and "annum" for year. The sequence of events in the chapters of Revelation 19-21 places the Millennium in this order of predictions.

1) The Return of Jesus – Ch. 19:11-23
2) The Millennial Kingdom – Ch. 20:1-10
3) The Final Judgment – Ch. 20:11-15
4) The New Heaven and New Earth – Ch. 21

Here is how Jesus reveals the Millennium to John in an open vision of Heaven:

"I saw thrones on which were seated those who had been given authority to judge. And I saw the souls of those who had been beheaded because of their testimony for Jesus and because of the word of God. They had not worshiped the beast or his image and had not received his mark on their foreheads or their hands. They came to life and reigned with Christ a thousand years. (The rest of the dead did not come to life until the thousand years were ended.) This is the first resurrection. Blessed and holy are those who have part in the first resurrection. The second death has no power over them, but they will be priests of God and of Christ and will reign with Him for a thousand years." (Rev 20:4-6)

For the first two centuries, the Christian Church accepted the idea of the Millennium as an earthly Kingdom that came in the exact sequence laid out in Revelation 19–21. Over time, however, a school of thought developed in the increasingly non-Jewish church where the Millennium of Revelation 20 became viewed as this present Church Age. This view was called Postmillennialism because Jesus returned at the *end* of the Millennial reign. "Post" is a prefix that means "after" and "pre" is a prefix that means "before". Postmillennialism and Premillennialism each have a major subset. Amillenialism is a more pessimistic version of Postmillennialism. The classic Premillennial view of the apostles and early church fathers is known today as Historic Premillenialism. It is distinguished from the more popular view which grew out of it known today as Dispensational Premillennialism. Here, in the historical order in which they appeared, are the four main views.

Historic Premillennialism sees Jesus coming to establish a literal thousand year global kingdom at His return, with Jerusalem as His likely capital city. He comes *before* the Millennium and *after* the period of great crisis called the Great Tribulation. This view is named "classic" or "historic" because it is the only millennial view found in the writings of the Church fathers of the first one and half centuries AD. It has also been called Covenant Premillennialism, because it is not in basic conflict with the Covenant Theology of the Reformed and Presbyterian tradition. It is also known as the Post-tribulation Premillennial view. Historic Premillennialism is consistent with the development of thought throughout the 66 books of the Bible and the earliest Christian tradition. I believe it was the consensus of the first generation of believers and will return as the consensus of the last.

Postmillennialism and **Amillennialism** hold that the Revelation 20:1-10 Millennial Reign began when Jesus birthed the Church after He rose from the dead and ascended to Heaven. The Millennial Reign is an invisible Kingdom. Postmillennialism and Amillennialism developed concurrently during the third to fifth centuries AD. Amillennialism, as a term, did not appear until around one hundred years ago. It may help you to understand what we call Postmillenialism today as "optimistic Postmillennialism" and what we call Amillennialism today as "pessimistic Postmillennialism." Both are postmillennial in the sense that the prefix "post" means "after". Jesus returns after the Millennium.

In optimistic Postmillennialism, the Church's government will spread until the world's cultures and institutions are fully Christianized. Then Jesus returns. The appeal of optimistic Postmillennialism is its confidence in the eventual triumph of the leadership of Jesus through the Church in this Age no matter how long it takes.

In pessimistic Postmillennialism, or Amillennialism, the triumph of the Church is less universal. There is room for a literal future Anti-Christ, Great Tribulation, and Great Apostasy. What we call Postmillennialism says Jesus returns to a saved Earth. Amillennialism says Jesus returns *to save* the Earth.

Dispensational Premillennialism divides God's redemptive action in history into seven dispensations (ways that God chooses to work with the human race) between creation and final judgment. The Millennial Kingdom is the last of those. Before the Millennium, the Church is secretly taken away to Heaven or "raptured" by Jesus before (or some say in the middle of) a final seven year period of tribulation. During this time God deals directly with ethnic Israel again. This view is vastly more popular than Historic Premillennialism today, but it lacks historic and philosophic continuity to the apostolic and early church. Dispensationalism appeared in 1830 with John Nelson Darby of the Plymouth Brethren movement in England as its main voice.

Affirming Our Unity

It is important for me to emphasize that even if your current eschatological view interprets many passages of biblical prophecy, the Millennial Kingdom, and the Throne Room of God as literary symbolism, it does not mean that you necessarily long for Jesus' return less than those who read the same text more literally. Christians with different views can love, and be loved by, Jesus just the same! It also doesn't mean that those with a more allegorical way of interpreting prophecy can't also have a powerful sense of the urgency of our moment of human history. Other biblical principles can give the honest, faithful Christian genuine motivation to live in intimacy with Jesus and a sense of the urgency of life.

Since then we know what it is to fear the Lord, we try to persuade men... For Christ's love compels us, because we are convinced that one died for all, and therefore all died. And He died for all, that those who live should no longer live for themselves but for Him who died for them and was raised again. (2 Cor. 5:11,14)

Anyone who has been touched by the Living Christ and has the Holy Spirit living in them has a new motivation for living among others. We can live passionate lives as His servants and messengers simply out of the fear of the Lord and the love of Jesus. It works! *All* readers of the Bible have the wonderful promise of a "Blessed Hope" in Titus 2:11-14:

For the grace of God that brings salvation has appeared to all men. It teaches us to say "No" to ungodliness and worldly passions, and to live self-controlled, upright and godly lives in this present age, while we wait for the blessed hope—the glorious appearing of our great God and Savior, Jesus Christ, who gave himself for us to redeem us from all wickedness and to purify for himself a people that are his very own, eager to do what is good.

A "Postmil" follower of Jesus may long for His glorious appearance as much as a "Premil" one. Postmils view the return of Jesus as a "period" instead of a "comma" in world history. Premils need to understand that Postmil brothers also believe God is coming to reign and rule with His saints on the Earth. But for them it comes in the New Heaven and New Earth. We may disagree on the application or sequence of the Millennium of Revelation 20, but we can all agree on the full restoration of Heaven and Earth in Revelation 21.

There are diagrams of the four views in the appendices. Refer to them as you read. They are the work of Dr. Jack Arnold, a beloved former pastor. Each view has had popular seasons over the last 2000 years. Each view has passionate, intelligent adherents in the global Church today. No matter what our view may be, it is wise for us all to admit that our historical, social, theological, and cultural contexts inevitably impact the way we read the Bible.

Some Amils and Postmils may be surprised to learn that there *is* a Premillennial alternative to the Dispensational view. It is easy to think Dispensationalism is the only Premil view because it has been the one promoted by Christian televangelists for decades. Its popularity at the grass roots level is fueled by prophecy conferences, movies, and books. Best-selling novels like Hal Lindsey's *Late Great Planet Earth* (1970) and the *Left Behind* series by Tim Lahaye and Jerry B. Jenkins (1995-2007) have been wildly successful at pitching a vision of the future where followers of Jesus escape global calamity under an Anti-Christ leader. In recent decades at the academic level, some traditional Dispensationalists have been moving toward a "Progressive Dispensationalism" that incorporates many aspects of Historic Premillennialism.

Our understanding of Bible prophecy and current events will grow clearer with the maturity of history itself. Future events could bring about a consensus of Millennial expectations like that of the early church. Since Millennial views tend to change with time, let's look back in history to see how Premillennialism first fell out of mainstream Church thinking.

Chapter 2

Historic Overview of Christian End Time Views

*"To bring all things in heaven and on earth together
under one head, even Christ"*
(Ephesians 1:10)

Why did Postmillennialism Eclipse Premillennialism?

The view that Jesus would return before establishing His Millennial Kingdom began drifting out of the center of Christian theology about 1800 years ago. But there were always some Christians who held a Post-tribulational, Premillennial view across history. Scientist Sir Isaac Newton, writer J. R. R. Tolkien of Hobbit fame, and culture critic and theologian Dr. Francis Schaeffer are a few recent standouts. Why did it fade from the majority?

1) Historical Changes - After the destruction of the Second Jewish Temple in 70 AD and the demise of national Israel in 135 AD, there was no national Israel to which the prophecies concerning a future Millennial Kingdom could literally apply. The Church Fathers interpretive methods for Bible passages concerning God's redemptive plans for Jews in a national Israel became increasingly spiritualized.

2) Shifting Theological Debates and Writings– Historic Premillennialism today is the closest thing to the Jewish-Christian millennial view held by early Church leaders before the writings of Clement and Origen around 230 AD.

David Pawson in his book *When Jesus Returns* writes:

"The early fathers believed in 'the corporeal reign of Christ on this very earth' (to quote Papias, bishop of Hierapolis in Asia). . . Many other names are cited as holding this 'pre-millennial" position – among them Barnabas, Hermas, Ignatius, Polycarp, Irenaeus, Justin Martyr, Tertullian, Hippolytus, Methodius, Commodian, and Lactantius" (p. 259)

Not every scholar would agree with Pawson that Hermas, Ignatius, and Polycarp belong on this list. Even so, the point is made that among the earliest Church Fathers who wrote about their eschatology, Premillennialism was the prevalent view.

Dan Gruber in his book, *The Church and the Jews – The Biblical Relationship* quotes Justin Martyr:

"But I and all the other entirely orthodox Christians, know that there will be a resurrection of the flesh, and also a thousand years in a Jerusalem built up and adorned and enlarged, as the prophets Ezekiel and Isaiah and all the rest acknowledge" (p. 277).

Though Justin Martyr envisioned a New Jerusalem, his generation did not envision a restored ethnic Israel as Premillennialists would today. He was not "pro-Israel" but "pro-Church."

Clement and Origen wrote from the Eastern Greek speaking church in Alexandria where idealistic Greek philosophy turned its nose up at the literalism of Hebraic thought. The Church was increasingly influenced by non-Jewish leaders and ways of thinking. The idea of a pure spiritual heaven as a final destination began to triumph over the prospect of an enduring, reunited Heaven and Earth under the leadership of Jesus. The Millennial Kingdom was negatively portrayed as sensual in Origen's letters. The Greek Church's philosophic preference for Heaven over a Messianic Kingdom on Earth may have been a concession to Gnosticism. The apostle John wrote against Docetism, a precursor of Gnosticism, the heresy that all things spiritual were good and all things material were bad.

Origen's strong rhetoric and personality started to make a literal Millennium look dirty. But it wasn't until the great theologian and church leader, Augustine, wrote *City of God* (between 413-426 AD) that Amillennialism and Postmillennialism had its decisive voice. Augustine's brilliance came at the right time as it gave a coherent historical and cultural interpretation of scripture within the new political reality of the acceptance of Christianity by the Roman Emperor Constantine after his conversion in 312 AD.

3) Growing Anti-Semitism

Christianity began as a sect of Judaism. Jewish authorities objected to the admission of Gentiles without accepting the Jewish Law of Moses. After the Jewish revolts against Rome (AD 66-73) and (AD 132-135), most Christians and Jews disassociated. Jewish Christians who did not support the revolts were seen as enemies of the Jewish State. From this time on, few Jews were converted to Christianity.

Over time, Christians "returned the favor" and viewed Jews as enemies of the Church. That is why Justin Martyr and other Church Fathers saw the Church completely replacing the Jews in a restored future Jerusalem. When Emperor Constantine gathered the bishops from all over the Byzantine Empire for the first general church council at Nicea in 325 AD, none of the Christian leaders from Jewish heritage were invited. Anti-Jewish decrees were issued at Nicea. The Roman Empire began legal discrimination of Jews until they were eventually deprived of all rights. This basic stalemate and crisis remained between the Church and Jews until Napoleon temporarily smashed the Catholic papacy during the French Revolution in 1798. Meanwhile, Jews were subjected to centuries of animosity, persecutions, forced conversions, and massacres at the hands of Christian states.

4) Eschatology Was a Sideline Issue in the Great Reformation

Since Christian movements over the centuries have drawn their views of Bible passages from key founders and prominent concepts during the period of their birth, those views, like time capsules, still determine how each movement views the ancient text today.

Martin Luther, a German monk, sparked the Great Reformation in 1513 by protesting 95 things he didn't like about Roman Catholic Church practice on the doors of Wittenburg's Cathedral. But Luther did little to change anti-Semitism in the Church, much less consider any future role God had of restoring a Messianic Kingdom from Jerusalem.

What dominated the center stage of thinking in the reformation was how to rescue the truths of salvation in Christ by grace alone, through faith alone, based on scripture alone from a corrupt institution with torture chambers for heretics. That led to centuries of theological streams in the Great Reformation, Radical Reformation, and the Catholic counter-reformation traditions.

The great voices of the Reformation from Martin Luther, to John Calvin, to John Wesley came to view the "little horn" of Daniel 7:8,21 and "Mystery Babylon" of Revelation 17:6 as referring to the institution of the Pope and Roman Church. They had a compelling case. The corrupt Roman Church *was* making "war on the saints" through centuries of inquisitions fitting the description in Daniel of the "little horn" arising in Europe. The anti-Christ spirit called "the Beast" in Revelation 13:2, & 7-8, described one who would rise to world-wide influence. To the Reformers, Mystery Babylon "drunk with the blood of the saints and with the blood of the martyrs of Jesus" was the Roman Church which decreed thousands of death sentences for those preaching a message of salvation by grace alone through faith alone in Jesus alone.

This type of application of End Time prophecies of the Bible to the 1260 year historical period between Justinian's decree (which gave the Roman Popes imperial powers in Europe in 538 AD to the fall of the Imperial Papacy to Napoleon in 1798) is called "Historism." Historism, like Preterism, fits into an Amillennial construct.

To understand more about this particular view read Steve Wohlberg's *End Time Delusions*.

Presbyterian and Reformed fellowships grow out of the theological and cultural worldview of Christians in England who drafted the Westminster Confession of Faith from 1642 to 1647. There were enough Premillennialists present for the Amillennial Scottish Divines to complain to the Assembly. Still, there was no serious attempt to re-evaluate eschatology wholesale. For one thing, there was no nation called Israel in the sleepy environs of Palestine. For another, Reformation Churches like their Catholic and Orthodox counterparts were still aligned with Nation-States in the tradition of Constantine. Fortunately, the Westminster Confession allowed for eschatological diversity of thought.

5) 1800's to Present - Divided Opinions Over the Significance of a Reborn Jewish State

Biblical eschatology did not become a serious topic again on any broad scale in Christianity until the 1800's with the emergence of Premillennial Bible conferences in England that spread to America. The fresh fascination with biblical passages that seemed to point to a future restoration of a national Israel gave popular support to a political dream of some Jews and pro-Jewish Christian advocates called "Zionism." A movement to recreate a national homeland for Jews in Palestine began to pick up steam.

For Jews, the hunger for a sovereign state in their ancient homeland was a felt need for the agnostic and secular Jew suffering politically as well as for the conservative Jews and Christians who were motivated by unfulfilled Bible prophecies of a Messianic Kingdom. The horror of the Nazi genocide against 6 million Jews in WWII concentration camps produced the moment of international political will necessary to create a home for global Jewry. The seemingly impossible happened with the rebirth of a political state for ethnic Jews called Israel in 1948.

Even with the stunning re-emergence of a Jewish nation, the Christian world was still divided across a broad spectrum as to what biblical significance this modern Israel held. The World Council of

Churches (a liberal leaning global assembly) acknowledged that the God of history was preserving the Jewish people for some future purpose. That idea still represents the broadest Christian consensus. The debate continues around questions of if, how, and when God will save ethnic Israel.

Chapter 3

Millennial Views of Israel

*"It is not the children by physical descent who are
God's children, but it is the children of the promise who are
regarded as Abraham's offspring."* (Romans 9:8)

Israel, the Church, and the End-Times

Historic Premillennialism, Amillennialism, and Postmillennialism affirm that Jesus created one new humanity of Jew and Gentile at the cross in such a way that the Church inherits the Old Covenant promises. Dispensational Premillennialism claims there is a plan where the Church is taken out of the earth in an early rapture while God deals with Israel separately during a future Great Tribulation.

The popularity of an eschatological view will shift depending on how that view syncs with developing historical events. A newly created Israel, as remarkable as it was, did not bring about an eschatological Christian consensus in 1948. Nor will a Third Jewish Temple, if built, automatically settle the debate. But suffice it to say that if the Church has not been raptured out of the earth and an Anti-Christ style global leader defiles a Third Jewish Temple as a great tribulation breaks out, the options narrow down. At that point only Amillennialism and Historic Premillennialism are left on the table.

Since biblical End Time scenarios are focused on Jerusalem and the future response of Jews, how we understand the Israel of the Old Testament, the Church of the New Testament, the rabbinical tradition of Judaism, and the modern political state of Israel today matters a great deal.

New Testament writers, especially Paul, saw the Church as the fulfillment of God's promise to make Israel a light to the Gentiles. Salvation was going out to all peoples from Israel through the Jewish Messiah, Jesus. The Temple System was now obsolete since the perfect blood of Jesus (as a final atonement for the sins of the world) replaced the blood of bulls and goats which were temporary. This new message of hope for eternal life and salvation from sin, while Hebrew in origin, spread through the world of its day.

Jesus Creates One New Man out of Jew and Gentiles

Jesus announced this transition in worship in a conversation with the Samaritan woman in John 4:21, 23:

"Woman," Jesus replied, "believe me, a time is coming when you will worship the Father neither on this mountain nor in Jerusalem. Yet a time is coming and has now come when the true worshipers will worship the Father in the Spirit and in truth, for they are the kind of worshipers the Father seeks."

Jesus knew that He would replace the Jewish Temple when He rose from the dead. As the Lord of all history, He knew that everything was about to change, because He *was* the change. In John's gospel, Jesus is not only presented in Jewish terms, but also in Greek. Jesus was the "Logos", Greek for "Word". Jesus was a Jewish man from Nazareth, but also the eternal Logos of God, uncreated deity, become flesh.

Since the Bible was written by Hebrews, understanding Jewish language, culture, and mindsets help unlock the mysteries of Bible prophecy. But what God did by sending His Son revolutionized both Jewish and Greek mindsets.

In Acts 15, the first Jewish leaders of the Church freed faith in Jesus from the Law of Moses and Jewish bound customs. Gentiles were not to be circumcised or required to keep the feasts and festivals prescribed in the Torah. God could be worshipped in Spirit and in Truth in countless cultural variations as long as they were just and righteous. This freedom to come to God through infinite cultural expressions is what has made global Christianity so dynamic and diverse. Jesus can be glorified in a Native American Christ centered dance just as much as in a Messianic Jewish Seder.

God's truth supersedes both Eastern and Western mindsets. Paul declares how the foolishness of a Messiah who offers Himself as the sin offering of the world offends *every* mindset, whether Jew or Greek.

Where is the wise person? Where is the teacher of the law? Where is the philosopher of this age? Has not God made foolish the wisdom of the world? For since in the wisdom of God the world through its wisdom did not know him, God was pleased through the foolishness of what was preached to save those who believe. Jews demand signs and Greeks look for wisdom, but we preach Christ crucified: a stumbling block to Jews and foolishness to Gentiles, but to those whom God has called, both Jews and Greeks, Christ the power of God and the wisdom of God. (I Corinthians 1:20-24)

God offends our minds to reveal our hearts. The pride of Jewish heritage or Greek wisdom won't cut it. Only the humility of following the leadership of Jesus through the Holy Spirit causes us to finish life and history well. Paul expresses this point in his letter to the Corinthian Church.

So from now on we regard no one from a worldly point of view. Though we once regarded Christ in this way, we do so no longer. Therefore, if anyone is in Christ, the new creation has come: The old has gone, the new is here! (2 Cor. 5:16-17)

I affirm the value of understanding Jewish roots as one would his family tree. It is fascinating! Knowing our dynamic past as a faith family also helps us know our exciting future. But the New Testament is clear that Gentiles do not need to become Jews to become followers of Jesus. Jesus, as a Jew, fulfills the Law of Moses and opens a new and living way through His body for all to come to God through Him.

Jesus fulfilled God's promise to Adam as the seed of the woman who would crush the head of the serpent. Jesus fulfilled God's promise to Abraham as the seed through whom the Gentiles would be blessed. Jesus fulfilled God's promise to David as the seed who would rule an everlasting unshakeable Kingdom. "For no matter how many promises God has made, they are "Yes" in Christ" (2 Cor. 1:20).

How do we view the modern nation of Israel?

Since the concept of the Church as spiritual successor to Old Covenant Israel is offensive to many Dispensationalists, it is not unusual to hear the term "Replacement Theology" used in a negative way to reference it. But the belief that the Church is "spiritual Israel" does not have to mean that one does not love Jewish people, respect the nation of Israel, or expect a stunning restoration of Jews as the Day of Lord approaches. In fact, Replacement Theology is not mainly about whether or not Jews and Gentiles became one new covenant people through the work of Jesus on the cross. That is basic Christianity.

The writer of Hebrews makes it plain that a New Covenant for Israel foretold in Jeremiah 31:31-34 was mediated by Jesus. Jesus' blood on the cross was a full and final atonement that super-ceded the temple priesthood sacrificial system instituted by God in the Covenant of Moses.

But in fact the ministry Jesus has received is as superior to theirs as the covenant of which he is mediator is superior to the old one, since the new covenant is established on better promises.

For if there had been nothing wrong with that first covenant, no place would have been sought for another. But God found fault with the people and said: "The days are coming, declares the Lord, when

I will make a new covenant with the people of Israel and with the people of Judah. It will not be like the covenant I made with their ancestors when I took them by the hand to lead them out of Egypt, because they did not remain faithful to my covenant, and I turned away from them, declares the Lord. This is the covenant I will establish with the people of Israel after that time, declares the Lord. I will put my laws in their minds and write them on their hearts. I will be their God, and they will be my people. No longer will they teach their neighbor, or say to one another, 'Know the Lord,' because they will all know me, from the least of them to the greatest. For I will forgive their wickedness and will remember their sins no more."

By calling this covenant "new," he has made the first one obsolete; and what is obsolete and outdated will soon disappear. (Hebrews 8:6-13)

Jesus fulfills, and thus replaces, the requirements of the Mosaic covenant and extends salvation from Israel to every nation. But the question remains as to whether Old Testament prophecies of a gloriously restored national Israel still apply to Jews today.

Jesus seems to have a restored national Israel in mind in a conversation with His disciples as He is about to fulfill the Old Covenant Passover meal by becoming the Passover Lamb.

"You are those who have stood by me in my trials. And I confer on you a kingdom, just as my Father conferred one on me, so that you may eat and drink at my table in my kingdom and sit on thrones, judging the twelve tribes of Israel" (Luke 22:28-30).

While the disciples who heard Jesus say this are with Him now in Heaven, this verse leaves the door open that the Kingdom Jesus inaugurated in His first coming will not be complete until He returns and establishes it from a restored Israel.

Amillennialism and Postmillennialism believe all prophecies of a restored national Israel are fulfilled in the Church in this Age.

Dispensational and Historic Premillennialism believe the land promises given to Abraham, and the Messianic Kingdom promises given to David, are fulfilled in the Millennium that follows Jesus' return. Many of God's promises in the Bible *are* fulfilled in the

Church Age. But the Millennial Kingdom is when all remaining prophecies are fulfilled.

Eastern Orthodox Churches would be one example of Replacement Theology. Since they believe all promises made to Old Testament saints are completed in the Church, there is no unique prophetic significance to the Israeli State in the Middle East today. That is one reason why Russia, with its Russian Orthodox majority, tends to side with Israel's political enemies, while the USA with its large population of pro-Israel Premillennial Christians has consistently been Israel's political ally.

Another view of Israel is the "Dual Covenant" theory. This view believes that Jews today may enter the Kingdom of God without accepting the leadership of Jesus as their Messiah. They are simply "God's chosen people" regardless of their response to the claims of Jesus to be their King or how they act toward other human beings. Radical Zionists who are conservative Christians hold this view along with liberal Christians who want to say that Jews should not be called to faith in Jesus because they are going to Heaven anyway.

Amil and Postmil Christians, with liberal Jews, are more willing to consider a political solution where a Palestinian state is created out of the land west of the Jordan. Premillennial Christians and Jewish Zionists are generally committed to resisting any such idea.

While extreme Zionists use the Bible to justify any political means to preserve a Jewish state in the Middle East today, Islamic Jihadists use the Qu'ran to justify any political means to destroy Israel to usher in the millennial vision of Islam. From a secular standpoint modern Israel has as much right to secure defensible, national borders as any nation. They have more reason than any nation to be vigilant against hostile neighbors. Islamic nations are eager for the right moment to re-conquer Palestine. The social, political, religious, and military scenarios prophesied in the apocalyptic writings of the Bible are ripening before our eyes.

Living in Tension

The question of how followers of Jesus ought to view Jews who reject Him as Messiah goes back to the New Testament Church.

There was great heartbreak over the division among Jews as a resurrected Jesus was preached in the first century world. Paul was torn in two because of the breach.

I speak the truth in Christ—I am not lying, my conscience confirms it through the Holy Spirit—I have great sorrow and unceasing anguish in my heart. For I could wish that I myself were cursed and cut off from Christ for the sake of my people, those of my own race, the people of Israel. (Romans 9:1-4)

A strong separation between those who accepted the leadership of Jesus and those who rejected it was inevitable and Jesus Himself predicted it.

Do you think I came to bring peace on earth? No, I tell you, but division. From now on there will be five in one family divided against each other, three against two and two against three. They will be divided, father against son and son against father, mother against daughter and daughter against mother, mother-in-law against daughter-in-law and daughter-in-law against mother-in-law. (Luke 12:51-52)

The claim of Jesus to be Israel's Messiah was controversial then and today. We would be mistaken to paper over that irreconcilable claim in order to make Jesus more palatable for Jews today. A biblical Christian must call every Jew to follow Jesus to be a part of the covenant family of God.

For there is no difference between Jew and Gentile—the same Lord is Lord of all and richly blesses all who call on him. (Romans 10:12)

If the Church as both Jew and Gentile is the spiritual descendent of Abraham by faith in his seed Jesus, then how do we regard global rabbinical Jewry and the modern nation of Israel? Is God preserving the Jewish people for some future purpose? I believe so. Is it a miracle of history that Israel exists as a national homeland for people of Jewish identity? I believe it is. The fact that a nation was reborn in

1948 for a persecuted people who had been wandering throughout the earth since 135 AD is simply amazing.

Does God care about the injustices committed by Zionist forces against the Arab Christian and Muslim residents of the land in the process of taking control of Palestine in 1947? Absolutely. God hates all injustice. There is still a deep wound in the heart of the Palestinian people over the means by which Jewish forces with the help of Western nations took control of lands that had been their homeland for centuries. Add poverty, political oppression, vain religion, racial prejudice, terrorism, media bias, and Islamic imperialism to the equation and you have the bleeding wound of hatred and fear we call the Middle East today. Naim Ateek is an Arab Palestinian Christian theologian whose book *Justice and Only Justice* is an important read for American Christians who have mostly turned a deaf ear to the cries of Palestinian brothers and sisters in Christ.

From a Premillennial view, there is no sustainable peace for the Middle East. All flesh is on a collision course with God Himself. The secular world is sadly overconfident that political compromise will resolve the issues. The conflict growing around Jerusalem will only be resolved when Jesus returns. His leadership alone will bring lasting peace. But that doesn't mean Christians should stop working for justice. God loves justice and delights in mercy.

The gospel of Jesus is not merely an offer of personal salvation, it is the surrender terms God offers mankind. It is both personal and political. We all have sinned. We all are saved by the same sacrifice Jesus made. The presence of the obedient Church on Earth is what brings global conflict to a peak. To pray for the "peace of Jerusalem" is to pray for the return of Jesus to establish His Kingdom of peace over the whole Earth.

There are two pressing questions for thinking Christians who pray for the peace of Jerusalem even as we prepare for cataclysmic events preceding the return of Jesus to that troubled city.

1) Is there a way to view political Israel as a prophetic sign of the return of Jesus, and affirm their national right to exist within secure borders, without condoning unjust policies employed toward non-Jews?

2) Will followers of Jesus love Jews around the world enough to share the love and truth of Jesus as Messiah even if it means appearing "anti-semitic".

All Israel Will Be Saved

All millennial views accept a restoration of Jews when they accept the leadership of Jesus. In the Historic Premillennial view, God's full restoration of Israel will occur just before, during, or immediately after, the return of Jesus with Heaven's armies. Those physical sons and daughters of Abraham who welcome the leadership of Jesus will marvel at their ancestors' unique role in God's plan to save all people who followed Messiah.

"The Redeemer will come to Zion, to those in Jacob who repent of their sins," declares the Lord.

This prophecy is given in Isaiah 59:20 six hundred years before Jesus fulfilled it.

But Isaiah 59:20 is repeated as *future* prophecy by Paul in Romans 11:26-27 *after* Jesus, the Redeemer *has* come to Zion: "And so all Israel will be saved, as it is written: 'The deliverer will come from Zion; he will turn godlessness away from Jacob. And this is my covenant with them when I take away their sins.'"

This Old Testament promise has a "near" fulfillment in the first coming of Jesus and Paul repeats Isaiah as a New Testament promise with a "far" fulfillment in Jesus' return. Promises like Isaiah 59:20 with dual fulfillments were how the Jewish apostles who founded the Church saw the covenant blessings in Jesus being extended to the world in the future. Israel remaining in the blessings of the covenant was conditional on their recognition of Jesus as God's Messiah Son. Even though most leaders of Israel rejected Jesus in His first coming, God remains faithful to His promises to Israel and will graft them back into the covenant family at the end of the Age.

God's covenant blessings are conditional even to His "chosen" people. He wants *voluntary* lovers. Eternity is a marriage, not a dictatorship. Citizenship in the Kingdom of God comes to anyone who says "yes" to God's chosen Bridegroom King, Jesus. The offer from Yahweh to Jew and Gentile alike is, "I have chosen my Son to lead the universe." Our status as chosen depends on our choice to follow Jesus.

Is it important to God that every Gentile believer honor Jews today whether they yet accept Jesus as Messiah or not? Yes, according to Paul in Romans 11:28: "Concerning the gospel they are enemies for your sake, but concerning election they are beloved for the sake of the fathers." God is zealous for the Jews of the world to come home to His heart again. He has a sovereign plan, still to be unfolded, where Israel's salvation comes simultaneously with salvation for the whole world.

For if you (Non-Jews) were cut out of the olive tree which is wild by nature, and were grafted contrary to nature into a cultivated olive tree, how much more will those who are natural branches, be grafted into their own olive tree? For I do not desire brethren, that you should be ignorant of this mystery, lest you should be wise in your own opinion, that blindness in part has happened to Israel until the fullness of the Gentiles has come in. And so all Israel will be saved.
(Romans 11:24-26)

Land and Feuding Families

I believe the current state of Israel is biblically significant. The existence of national Israel is a witness to God's faithful promise keeping across the generations. But it is important not to forget that this current political Israel is yet a forerunner to the future Millennial Kingdom. That coming Kingdom will be the unmistakable fulfillment of Bible prophecy and God's promises to Abraham's descendants. If the land promises given by God to Abraham will only be fulfilled in the Millennial Kingdom, then applying the Genesis 13:14-17, Genesis 15:18-21, and 17:8-9 land promises to today's politics only creates confusion, perpetuates injustice, and drives Jews and Arabs further from the good news of the leadership of Jesus.

The Jews of today AND the Arabs of today were in Abram's body when God first declared that his descendants would be given the physical land where the political nations of Israel, Egypt, Jordan,

Lebanon, Iraq, and Syria exist today. Jews and Arabs are both Semitic people, the name given to descendants of Noah's son Shem. But while Arabs and Jews can trace genealogical lines to Abraham, they do so through different sons. Ishmael was the product of Abraham's union with his wife's maidservant, Hagar. God's covenant blessings would come not through the line of Ishmael, but through Abraham's child of promise, Isaac. Isaac was born to Sarah well past her childbearing years when Ishmael was 13. Isaac was the miraculous fulfillment of God's promise to provide Abraham with a son who would carry the covenant promises to bless all peoples. Abraham's blessing came to all men through Jesus.

He redeemed us in order that the blessing given to Abraham might come to the Gentiles through Christ Jesus, so that by faith we might receive the promise of the Spirit. (Galatians 3:14)

The three monotheistic faiths—Judaism, Christianity, and Islam—all claim Abraham as Father and all stake competing claims to the real estate of the Middle East. The Crusades of the Middle Ages were a Postmillennial application of eschatology. In order for Christendom to advance territorially a military conquest of the Holy Land was necessary. This brought devastating results to Jews, Christians, and Muslims alike.

Jews, Christians, and Muslims are as driven by political ideologies today as ever before. In the case of Islam, Muslim nation states created by force are entirely justified by the Quran and by the example of Muhammad. Use of military force was not only sanctioned by the founder of Islam but promoted whenever expedient. Any honest reading of history and today's newspapers will bear this out.

In the case of the Jews, Israel may exist as a political reality, but it exists without a Third Temple on the site of the earlier two. Unless a Third Temple is built, it is impossible for Orthodox Jews to entirely fulfill the Law of Moses. That Law still requires temple priests and animal sacrifices. Without that centerpiece of national identity operating for nearly two thousand years, the Judaism of rabbinic tradition meanders between extremes of atheistic secular humanism and ultra-conservative zealotry. While I agree that the creation of a Jewish homeland in the British Protectorate of Palestine in 1948 was a sign pointing to the nearness of the fulfillment of biblical prophecy, I would suggest that the real "mega-sign" of the countdown to the return of Jesus is the establishment of a Third Jewish Temple on the Jerusalem Temple Mount.

The Blessing Given to Abraham

Christian Zionism applies the promise God gave to Abram in Genesis 12:3 to "Bless those who bless you and curse those who curse you" directly to the modern Israel of today. It is important to note that Abram at the time the blessing was given was not a Jew or Israelite. He was a Chaldean who preceded his grandson, Jacob, renamed Israel, and Jacob's fourth son, Judah, from whom we get the term Jew. Because the Israel of the Old Testament and the Israel of today share a name, it is easy to confuse the two as equivalent. Depending on one's view, the blessing of Genesis 12:3 is either for the global Church or national Israel. Dispensational Premillennialism grew up in the 1800's alongside the Zionist political movement in England and directly applies Genesis 12:3 to the political state.

If the God of Heaven and Earth punished *biblical* Israel for oppressing the poor, denying justice to the alien, and rejecting their Messiah, then how is that same God of justice likely to treat *political* Israel today if she sheds innocent blood and remains in rejection toward God's appointed Leader for them?

There need be no doubt how to apply the Genesis 12:3 blessing of Abraham today. Paul applies Genesis 12:3 directly to the Church consisting of both Jew and Gentile.

The Scripture foresaw that God would justify the Gentiles by faith, and announced the gospel in advance to Abraham: "All nations will be blessed through you." So those who have faith are blessed along with Abraham, the man of faith. There is neither Jew nor Greek, slave nor free, male nor female, for you are all one in Christ Jesus.

If you belong to Christ, then you are Abraham's seed, and heirs according to the promise. (Galatians 3:8,9, 28, 29)

Paul sees the New Covenant church as spiritual inheritors of the blessing given Abraham. All people may now become co-heirs of all the spiritual blessings of Abraham through His Seed, Jesus Christ. Paul teaches in his letter to the church in Ephesus that Jesus made one new humanity of Jew and Gentile through his blood sacrifice on the cross.

For he himself is our peace, who has made the two one and has destroyed the barrier, the dividing wall of hostility, by abolishing in his flesh the law with its commandments and regulations. His purpose was to create in himself one new man out of the two, thus making peace, and in this one body to reconcile both of them to God through the cross, by which he put to death their hostility. (Ephesians 2:14-16)

The sacrifice of Jesus created access to God for all people. Anyone may now, by trusting Jesus as Messiah, inherit the blessings given to Abraham. This global invitation does not nullify the promise of a future restoration of Abraham's physical offspring. To say that there is no plan for ethnic Israel is to forget what is promised in Romans 11:26. . . "All Israel will be saved."

The promise of Romans 11:26 applies to a future generation of Jews who will welcome Jesus. The Jews of today will give birth to those future leaders of Jerusalem. God is keeping His promise to make Jerusalem the "praise of the whole earth" when it is the City of the Great King in the Millennial Kingdom. God has a special plan for Israel, but it is not a separate plan. It is important to honor Jews and national Israel today in a way that does not show an unbiblical favoritism toward their politics or turn a blind eye to injustice. To love Israel should not mean hatred toward her political enemies who are also objects of God's promises and love in the gospel of Jesus Christ.

*But do not forget this one thing, dear friends: With the Lord a day is like a thousand years, and a thousand years are like a day. The Lord is not slow in keeping his promise, as some understand slowness. He is patient with you, not wanting **anyone** to perish, but **everyone** to come to repentance.* (2 Peter 3:8-9)

Do not hold the faith of our Lord Jesus Christ, the Lord of Glory with partiality. (James 2:1)

God blesses justice, righteousness, and truth. He does not put *any* political nation or ethnic group on an automatic divine pedestal. God's plan is to cause Jews to want the covenant blessings they see flowing through Jesus to the Church.

Jesus rebuked His hometown synagogue for thinking themselves superior to other peoples in His first sermon in Luke 4:24-27:

"I tell you the truth," he continued, "no prophet is accepted in his hometown. I assure you that there were many widows in Israel in Elijah's time, when the sky was shut for three and a half years and there was a severe famine throughout the land. Yet Elijah was not sent to any of them, but to a widow in Zarephath in the region of Sidon. And there were many in Israel with leprosy in the time of Elisha the prophet, yet not one of them was cleansed—only Naaman the Syrian."

Jesus was saying that the God of Israel was the God of every people. His love extends to the Gentiles. Their response to His message?

All the people in the synagogue were furious when they heard this. They got up, drove him out of the town, and took him to the brow of the hill on which the town was built, in order to throw him down the cliff. (Luke 4:28-29)

Jesus was not politically or theologically correct in their view. He eventually died as an enemy of the Jewish and Roman state.

Not of This World

The God of Israel in the Old Testament is the God who "loves justice" (Isaiah 61:8) and sent Jesus to establish justice through the blood of the cross between God and every ethnic group.

When Jesus was asked by the Roman governor Pilate if He was a King, Jesus replied, "My Kingdom is not of this world, if it were my disciples would fight for me." (John 18:36)

Jesus rules a Kingdom now from Heaven through the prayers and faith-born actions of his followers that cannot be contained in a political movement or national boundary. The culture of the Kingdom of God always has political implications. Yet Christianity is not primarily a political movement and inevitably suffers when ties to political systems of this Age are forged too strongly. All of the kingdoms of this age are marked for destruction or redemption including the current states of Israel and the United States of America. The Kingdom we are citizens of has not yet fully appeared.

Chapter 4

Comparing Premillennial Views

"Do your best to present yourself to God as a workman who does not need to be ashamed and who correctly handles the word of truth." (2 Timothy 2:14)

Premillennialism Makes a Comeback

L et's revisit our timeline of End Time views. From Augustine in the fifth century until the present, Amillennialism and Postmillennialism have been the default eschatology of the global Church. Premillennialism began to gain ground again in the nineteenth century.

For decades during the 1800s, Post-tribulationists and Pretribulationists met together at Bible Conferences in Britain and America. Their common Premillennialism held them together, but later disagreements split the camps. Dispensationalism grew more popular, especially when the Scofield Study Bible was first published in 1909. Notes and commentary were written around the text of Scofield's Bible that many readers assumed were as true as the Scriptures themselves.

Dispensationalists made strong distinctions between the way God worked with Jews and the Church. The Church was a Plan B for God resulting from Israel's national rejection of Jesus' leadership. God would remove the Church completely from the world in a future rapture event in order to restart the prophetic clock for seven more years with Israel before the return of Christ.

Historic Premillennialists emphasized the unity of God's redemptive plan throughout the Old and New Testaments. The Covenant theology of the Reformed and Presbyterian Churches was compatible with the Historic Premillennnial view but not with the Dispensationalist view with its separate program of salvation for Jews. For Reformation thinkers, the Church of Christ was an extension of Old Testament Israel—not a Plan B.

The theory that Jesus comes invisibly to take His Church to Heaven before the tribulation was not convincing for many Premillennialists as Dispensationalism grew. Though the rapture of the Church before the tribulation is widely taught and believed today, opponents still find no compelling argument in Scripture for what has become a major popular doctrine. One pitfall of the early rapture theory is that it does not prepare the Bride of Christ to embrace the fire of martyrdom and miracles during the waves of the Great Falling Away, Great Tribulation, and the Great Harvest just before the return of Jesus.

Historic Premillennialists insist Jesus does not take His followers out of the world during the last seven years prior to His coming. God *wants* Jesus followers from every nation in the world because they are the ones agreeing with His leadership until He comes. It is the presence of the Church which *produces* the confrontations. They are the ones on Earth praying down the Heavenly judgments God sends on Satan's leaders during the Great Tribulation period. Though the Anti-Christ will horribly persecute the Bride of Christ, it is the very same suffering Bride who will cry out for God to send justice through the conquering leadership of Jesus. The praying persecuted global church and a turning of Jews to Jesus as Messiah is what causes God to send Jesus back as the Bridegroom King and Judge.

The story of God's deliverance of Israel as a nation from the tyranny of Egypt's Pharaoh is a paradigm for the future Church under a Global Anti-Christ. God heard the 400 year outcry of His enslaved people and sent them a deliverer in Moses. Israel remained in Egypt during the ten supernatural judgments sent by God. The judgments announced by Moses fell on the Egyptians, but not on the Hebrews who lived in Goshen. God supernaturally protected His covenant people as a witness to Himself. However, the natural suffering of the Hebrews increased during God's judgments because Pharaoh increased their persecution as his slaves. Historic Premillennialists believe the future Church will experience great supernatural protection in the midst of great persecution.

Dispensationalists look forward to *escaping* the tribulation. Historic Premillennialists anticipate *shining* for Jesus *during* the tribulation. The faithful, persecuted Church is the *mature Church*. The Pretribulation Rapture theory implies a different view of suffering than one where the Church is given the grace of perseverance and divine protection to endure through tribulation.

Suffering and Death

It might seem depressing that God's people are not exempt from the Great Tribulation, but biblical suffering is never without purpose. It is an honor to live in the generation of Jesus' return and should not be seen any other way. Jesus referred to those who are persecuted for His sake as "blessed." The rewards for overcoming great suffering are eternal. God gives grace not merely to avoid suffering but to endure it and triumph through it.

No one looks forward to pain and suffering. It is no wonder that the view of Jesus coming for His Bridal people *after* the Great Tribulation is less popular than the view of believers being transported to safe ground *before* the Big One comes.

Dispensationalists rightly insist God's people do not suffer the anger of God in His End Time judgments. However, God's people *do* suffer the anger of men and the loving *discipline* of God in every generation, including the last. I believe there will be many miraculous ways in which God protects, delivers, and sustains the Church during Great Tribulation before the return of the Messiah. But I also do not expect that God's people will be completely exempt from earthquakes, famines, plagues, and wars, if the newspaper and history are any indication. Christians suffer and die like all men. But anyone whose trust is in Jesus has a hope of life to come that trumps the natural human fear of calamity, disease, and death.

When Jesus was questioned about whether Jews who died by persecution or natural disaster were less righteous than others, this is what He said:

Now there were some present at that time who told Jesus about the Galileans whose blood Pilate had mixed with their sacrifices. Jesus answered, "Do you think that these Galileans were worse sinners than all the other Galileans because they suffered this way? I tell you, no! But unless you repent, you too will all perish. Or those eighteen who died when the tower in Siloam fell on them—do you think they were more guilty than all the others living in Jerusalem? I tell you, no! But unless you repent, you too will all perish." (Luke 13:1-5)

Jesus was stating that accidents, natural disasters, and persecutions can befall anyone in the sovereignty of God. That by itself does not mean one person is less favored than another. The point Jesus is making is that life is short. Make sure you are in agreement with God your judge now. The greater issue is not dying the first death. All men statistically have that one coming. It is the second death that comes from suffering the judgment of God for eternity that we really need to be most concerned about. THAT is the wrath of God. Judgments are actually the mercy of God to give us incentives to turn to Him.

It is ironic to think that the first generation of followers who experienced great power, growth, AND great persecution would teach their generation, or by implication, future generations to expect *NOT* to suffer. Persevering in faith, *while* suffering for the name of Jesus, was the obvious teaching and example of the first leaders of the church. Church pioneers, Paul and Barnabas, said this to the new believers after Paul had been stoned and left for dead a few days before:

We must go through many hardships to enter the kingdom of God. (Acts 14:22)

It is important to note the words "must" and "many." Persevering through suffering is basic Christianity.

There are plenty of examples of when God supplied angelic rescues for His suffering servants. We just need to hold those biblical events in tandem with the examples of death God's servants were given to glorify Him. Peter and Paul got busted out of jail by angels, but John the Baptist had his head handed to King Herod on a platter and Peter and Paul met similar fates later. Their rescues were temporary.

How we finish our race of faith in death is a big deal. God says tested faith is more precious to Him than gold. If you read Scripture closely, our Father seems to require *more* suffering for those of His kids He is *most* intimate with. His One and Only Son is the prime case. Why is that? Is He mean? Is He evil? Or is He producing something so amazing and of such great value inside of the human heart that only the narrow gate of prayer and suffering will extract the last sacred drop of true love?

Premillennialism and Global Politics

Ideas have consequences. Because Christ-followers have influence, End Time biblical interpretations impact world politics. This is especially true in the case of efforts to work for (or not work for) peace in the Middle East. We surveyed some political views in the last chapter. But it is important to make one more distinction between how Historic Premils and Dispensational Premils view politics in the Middle East.

This verse from a psalm of David is an often repeated call to prayer that seems destined to be fulfilled only when His Messiah Son rules from there: "Pray for the peace of Jerusalem: May those who love you be secure. May there be peace within your walls and security within your citadels" (Ps. 122:6-7). Since that psalm was written three thousand years ago, there has been anything but peace in Jerusalem. It truly can lay claim to be the most fought over city in history.

One may object, "Why work for justice and peace in the Middle East if we can never fully achieve it?" One might as well ask, "Why have doctors? Why try to save a sick or wounded person from dying?" Or, "Why stand against the stampede of moral decline in American culture?"

Every human being is sacred because we all bear God's image in creation. Every person is accountable for their actions. People in authority face a greater punishment or reward. Every act of righteousness will be rewarded by God in the Age to come.

Dispensationalists, because of the early rapture theory, have to battle the tendency to disengage from social reformation in this world "because it is all going to burn and we won't be here when it does." Many Dispensationalists do not apply the cultural mandate or social ethics of Jesus' teachings in the Sermon on the Mount to the Church of today. But the Premillennialism of the early Christians didn't keep them from sifting through garbage heaps to find the babies thrown there by Romans exercising the legal right of infanticide. They knew God wanted to find them working for justice when the Lord returned.

Premillennialists today need to live as if every act of mercy and justice sown continues in some way into the Millennial Kingdom. If we believe that whatever is true, just, and righteous in redeemed people, nations, and institutions will continue into the Millennial Age we have a more deeply rooted biblical motivation to work for justice even as the Day of the Lord draws near.

Chapter 5

Interpreting Prophecy

"You know how to interpret the appearance of the sky,
but you cannot interpret the signs of the times."
(Matthew 16:3)

Same Data, Different Perspectives

I love lightning and thunder storms. I learned to love them at the age of six while sitting under a quilt on the parsonage porch. My Dad led a church in a little North Carolina town at the time. We had a grassy field across the street. Sometimes when dark thunderheads rolled over, my Dad, my sister, and I would enjoy the natural sound and light show bundled in blankets snuggling against each other's trembling bodies. The torrents of water falling off the roof of the porch misting over our laughing faces punctuated by loud cracks of thunder only added to our excitement.

Since then, weather channels with their Doppler radars and Storm Team coverage have injected more fear of tornados and destruction into my own family's home. Instead of blissful entertainment and family bonding on the porch, we keep an anxious eye on the various colors and currents on the TV screen, ready to flee to the basement at the sound of the tornado siren.

Excitement or fear? Storms can elicit both depending on your perspective. The biblical view of human history is that a Perfect

Storm is coming to the planet that *everyone* will have to endure. Is the world ending? Or is the world beginning?! Now is the time to choose how to view the same events that will unfold before billions of eyes. Now is the time to understand the prophecies of the Bible concerning the dramatic future of our global family.

When Does Prophecy End?

The apostle Paul gets a really bad rap for being too intellectual sometimes. But this is the same guy who wrote the "love" chapter of 1 Corinthians 13. What would weddings be without that famous ode to love?! While the best thing about the chapter is the priority of loving God and loving people above all cool spiritual gifts and heroic acts of social justice, it also says important things about prophecy:

Love never fails. But where there are prophecies, they will cease; where there are tongues, they will be stilled; where there is knowledge, it will pass away. For we know in part and we prophesy in part, but when perfection comes, the imperfect disappears. (1 Corinthians 13:8-12)

Trust me, the love part is the best! But now is the time for some theological terms for those interested in the question of "When does prophecy end?"

A person who believes all End Time prophecy was fulfilled with the coming of Jesus and with the destruction of the Jewish Temple in 70 AD is called a **Preterist**.

A person who believes End Time prophecy was partially fulfilled in the coming of Jesus and in the destruction of the Second Jewish Temple in 70 AD, but that End Time prophecy is yet to be fulfilled is called a **Futurist**.

In simple terms, Preterists read End Time prophecies as being fulfilled in the first generation of the Church and Futurists read End Time prophecies as being fulfilled in the last generation of the Church. Go to Appendix 6 for more explanation of these methods of interpretation and how they are applied to the Book of Revelation.

Premillennialists believe that prophecies of a gloriously restored national Israel will be fulfilled in the Millennial Kingdom after Jesus returns. Postmils and Amils believe that all prophecies of a restored Israel are fulfilled during this present Church Age before the return of Jesus. This view is sometimes called **Finalism** or **Realized Eschatology**.

The New Testament Spiritual Gift of Prophecy

End Time prophecy is different from the spiritual gift of prophecy that is listed among other gifts given by the Holy Spirit to New Testament believers in Romans 12 and 1 Corinthians 12. For the best treatment of the difference between prophecy in the Old Testament and prophecy in the New Testament, I recommend Dr. Wayne Grudem's book, *The Gift of Prophecy in the New Testament and Today*. The New Testament spiritual gift of prophecy is for the comfort, encouragement, and exhortation of others, not primarily for predicting the future.

A **Non-charismatic** Christian believes that the "spectacular" spiritual gifts given by the Holy Spirit to the early church (including prophecy, healing, miracles, dreams, visions, speaking in other tongues, etc. in the New Testament) ceased when the canon of the 66 Books of the Bible were finalized around AD 363 to 397. They believe all prophetic gifts ceased because they were only necessary to authenticate the true Church until the Bible was completed. For them, the canonized Bible is considered to be the "when perfection comes" part of 1 Corinthians 13:9. They are also called **Cessationists** since they believe certain gifts have ceased.

A **Charismatic** Christian believes that the spectacular spiritual gifts, including prophecy, still function in the Body of Christ today. A responsible charismatic does not put prophetic gifts today above the authority of the canonized Bible. That is, God still speaks directly to believers, but not in a way that is inconsistent with the content of the Bible. God's Spirit living in every believer loves to "speak" and reveal to them more of Jesus and how to live each day. The gift of prophecy for the charismatic, or "non-cessationist," ends when Jesus returns.

According to Paul's next verses in 1 Corinthians 13, there is a growing understanding on a personal level and a growing understanding on a historical level as we approach the future that God is authoring. History will conform to the Biblical narrative more and more clearly as time itself matures.

When I was a child, I talked like a child, I thought like a child, I reasoned like a child. When I became a man, I put childish ways behind me. Now we see but a poor reflection as in a mirror; then we shall see face to face. Now I know in part; then I shall know fully, even as I am fully known. (1 Cor. 13:11-12)

Isaiah 24 - A Case Study for Interpreting Bible Prophecy

Understanding Bible prophecy is *not* easy. Everyone comes with theological presuppositions which determine how they understand the words they read. Those who believe that much of what Old Testament prophets like Daniel, Jeremiah, Isaiah, and David have to say still applies to our children have some work to do. There is a rigorous academic side to this task. But it is do-able and rewarding with God's help and good teachers. Let's work with one key passage as an example.

Isaiah Chapter 24 is not a happy scene. The message of coming destruction by Isaiah the prophet applied to the Jewish audience of his day who would indeed experience the devastation he foretells in the Babylonian invasion. But Isaiah uses language that we do well to heed for our generation as well. One question is whether Isaiah's references to the whole earth are literal or figurative. Another is whether Chapter 24 is fulfilled in 586 BC when Jerusalem was sacked or if there is still an imbedded prophecy of things to come? How would you interpret these first six verses? Literal and/or figurative? Past and/or future?

See, the LORD is going to lay waste the earth and devastate it; he will ruin its face and scatter its inhabitants-it will be the same for priest as for people, for master as for servant, for mistress as for maid, for seller as for buyer, for borrower as for lender, for debtor as for creditor.

The earth will be completely laid waste and totally plundered. The LORD has spoken this word.

The earth dries up and withers, the world languishes and withers, the exalted of the earth languish. The earth is defiled by its people; they have disobeyed the laws, violated the statutes and broken the everlasting covenant. Therefore a curse consumes the earth; its people must bear their guilt. Therefore earth's inhabitants are burned up, and very few are left.

It is difficult not to get the idea of a universal or global devastation of the Earth. The devastation that happened in 586 BC was national. So is the message of Isaiah a part of something behind us or in front of us in the human story? Is it to be interpreted symbolically or literally?

We are given a clear reason for *why* the devastation comes. Judgment comes as a result of people breaking the "everlasting covenant" with Him. Does this only apply to God's covenant people, the Jews, or to all people today? Are a few survivors on a toasted planet the picture of the Earth at the end of this Age? These are difficult questions for any student of the Bible. It is why many people never attempt to study passages like these:

In that day the LORD will punish the powers in the heavens above and the kings on the earth below. They will be herded together like prisoners bound in a dungeon; they will be shut up in prison and be punished after many days. The moon will be abashed, the sun ashamed; for the LORD Almighty will reign on Mount Zion and in Jerusalem, and before its elders, gloriously.

One could say that these words only apply to the restoration of Israel after the captivity in Babylon and Persia. The Lord's punishment then did include contending with the dark powers that operate spiritually over human kingdoms. The sun and moon may be representative of the "powers in the heavens above" which are real spiritual powers that operate through human agents and mindsets. The powerful empires of the whole world known to Isaiah that ravaged tiny Israel *are* no more, so in some sense the prophecy is fulfilled. So, is the case closed? Or was the experience of Israel a forerunner for a future or final generation? Do the "powers of heaven" include Satan and the one third of Heaven he led in rebellion (according to Judeo-Christian tradition) against God before we were even created?

With the perspective of historical hindsight, Christians believe the LORD *did* come to Mount Zion and Jerusalem in the person of Jesus of Nazareth. The elders of the nation had Him killed as a *false* messiah in 33AD. Now, we have an unfulfilled part of this passage about the LORD governing all the powers of the Earth from Jerusalem. Is that referring to a Millennial Kingdom mentioned in Revelation 20 where Satan and the demonic horde that have ruled over us are bound for a thousand years?

And I saw an angel coming down out of heaven, having the key to the Abyss and holding in his hand a great chain. He seized the dragon, that ancient serpent, who is the devil, or Satan, and bound him for a thousand years. He threw him into the Abyss, and locked and sealed it over him, to keep him from deceiving the nations anymore until the thousand years were ended. After that, he must be set free for a short time.

I saw thrones on which were seated those who had been given authority to judge. And I saw the souls of those who had been beheaded because of their testimony for Jesus and because of the word of God. They had not worshiped the beast or his image and had not received his mark on their foreheads or their hands. They came to life and reigned with Christ a thousand years. (Rev. 20:1-4)

Every generation since Isaiah has had these same words of warning of great devastation. One option is to ignore them. Another is to idealize the prophecies as metaphor and lump them into a literary genre that should not be taken literally. Another is to interpret them in a way that concludes they no longer apply. But I hope you will accept the challenge of living with a potentially literal and future interpretation of Isaiah while discerning our own generation. If passages like Isaiah 24 and Revelation 20 apply to our times, we need to have the wisdom and courage to keep asking God what they mean. Don't give up! (For an excellent treatment of the Premillennial view of Isaiah 24 go to www.walterckaiserjr.com, the website of Dr. Walter Kaiser, President Emeritus of Gordon-Conwell Theological Seminary. Click on "Israel and Premillennialism".)

We have looked at an explicit prophetic word of an Old Testament prophet. Another kind of Bible prophecy is less explicit. Some Bible passages are viewed as prophetic *antetypes* or *foreshadowings* of things to come. One example would be how the life of someone in the Old Testament is a forerunner of the Messiah to come. This kind of prophecy isn't necessarily apparent until one is looking backward after a fulfillment or partial fulfillment, but it is still a credible witness to the prophetic nature of the Bible's inspiration.

Joseph as a Forerunner for Jesus

The Genesis story of Joseph, who was rejected and sold into slavery by his brothers, foreshadows how Jesus was rejected and killed by his Jewish brothers. Joseph's brothers had given him up as dead after they had thrown him into a pit and then sold him as a slave. When Joseph is revealed to them many years later, he has risen to the very right hand of Pharaoh in Egypt. God was actually training Joseph through prison, obscurity, and hardship to become the deliverer of the whole known world in a time of great crisis.

All Israel sought refuge from years of severe famine by leaving Canaan and traveling to the Egyptian superpower. Joseph reveals himself to his brothers from His position of authority. The reason they wanted to kill him as a boy was their hatred of his claim that they would one day bow to him. Now, there they are, bowing before him and wondering how he will treat them now! Instead of seeking revenge, Joseph weeps as he himself realizes that "You intended to harm me, but God intended it for good to accomplish what is now being done, the saving of many lives!" (Gen 50:20).

Descendents of Israel today are discovering that Y'eshua (the Hebrew way of saying Jesus), though He was the brother they rejected because of the offense of His claims of Messianic authority and declaration of the obsolescence of the temple sacrifice system, is indeed God's appointed Leader. That revelation will be the surprise plot twist of the Age for those Jews who are waiting for their Messiah to appear.

Zechariah the Jewish prophet says:

And I will pour out on the house of David and the inhabitants of Jerusalem a spirit of grace and supplication. They will look on me, the one they have pierced, and they will mourn for him as one mourns for an only child, and grieve bitterly for him as one grieves for a firstborn son. On that day the weeping in Jerusalem will be great. . . On that day a fountain will be opened to the house of David and the inhabitants of Jerusalem, to cleanse them from sin and impurity. (Zech 12:10-11, 13:1)

Imagine how bittersweet it will be for all Israel to realize that the one they rejected many centuries before was indeed their Messiah brother who loves them and has been working out a way to save them all at just the right time.

Jesus was rejected by the elders of Israel in the first century because He was not seen as fulfilling their understanding of the Messianic promises regarding the restoration of the political Kingdom of David. That huge issue was on the minds of his first disciples as they talked on the Mount of Olives before Jesus ascended to Heaven after the resurrection.

Restoring the Kingdom

In my former book, Theophilus, I wrote about all that Jesus began to do and to teach until the day he was taken up to heaven, after giving instructions through the Holy Spirit to the apostles he had chosen. After his suffering, he presented himself to them and gave many convincing proofs that he was alive. He appeared to them over a period of forty days and spoke about the kingdom of God. (Acts 1:1-3)

One might presume there would be little misunderstanding in the minds of the apostles about the nature of the Kingdom of God if the resurrected Jesus had been dialoging with them about it for 40 days. But they still had a question:

So when they met together, they asked him, "Lord, are you at this time going to restore the kingdom to Israel?" He said to them: "It is not for you to know the times or dates the Father has set by his own authority. But you will receive power when the Holy Spirit comes on you; and you will be my witnesses in Jerusalem, and in all Judea and Samaria, and to the ends of the earth." (Acts 1:6-8)

Jesus' answer was, "Stay tuned!" Everything was about to change with Jesus' ascension to Heaven and the sending of the Holy Spirit. The creation of the Church and the apostles' understanding of the Kingdom it served, was going to change as Luke records. By Acts 10 Gentiles are being added to the New Covenant community which spurs a leadership council in Jerusalem in Acts 15 to figure out how to deal with the new multi-cultural reality that the Holy Spirit was creating as the Gospel of Jesus spread.

The Messianic Kingdom began with the ascension of Jesus to the Throne of God right after their question. But if the current reign of Jesus from Heaven was the answer to their question, "Are you **at this time** going to restore the Kingdom to Israel?" why didn't Jesus say so? If the disciples question is valid, the restoration of the Kingdom to Israel is different from the current Messianic Kingdom and is still expected at the return of Jesus. The Messianic Kingdom includes both this current Church Age and the future Millennial Reign, but the Millennium is when that promise is kept.

Jesus wanted His followers to partner with Him on the task at hand, which was to tell His story to the whole world. The plan of God to have Kingdom citizens from every tongue and tribe and nation would require time and willing human vessels filled with His Spirit to carry out. That glorious responsibility is still ours who miss Him and want Him back. Prophecy in the Bible foretells the future, but not in a way that dictates it. God delights in partnering with His friends and empowering them to accomplish His purposes.

When God exercises full sovereignty over all human affairs, He does not violate free will in the process. The God of the Bible knows full well the outcome and climax of creation and history. So what is the point of thousands of years of conflict and drama if God already knows "the end from the beginning?" I believe He is redeeming sons and daughters from everywhere who, by His grace, will *freely* choose to love and serve Him. He desires voluntary lovers, and lots of them, because that is the kind of Lover He is. At the Cross He proved He was not willing to do His life without ours!

Returning to the Father

After he said this, he was taken up before their very eyes, and a cloud hid him from their sight.

They were looking intently up into the sky as he was going, when suddenly two men dressed in white stood beside them. "Men of Galilee," they said, "why do you stand here looking into the sky? This same Jesus, who has been taken from you into heaven, will come back in the same way you have seen him go into heaven." (Acts 1:9-11)

The ascension of Jesus is witnessed by people but the results were not. The resurrection is the reverse. No person witnessed life coming back into Jesus' cold body in the sealed tomb, but many witnessed the results. At the ascension, angels announce to the disciples where Jesus has gone and that He will return in the same way.

The prophet Daniel had a prophetic vision of what was to take place when Jesus re-entered Heaven as a Son of Man:

In my vision at night I looked, and there before me was one like a son of man, coming with the clouds of heaven. He approached the Ancient of Days and was led into his presence. He was given authority, glory and sovereign power; all nations and peoples of every language worshiped him. His dominion is an everlasting dominion that will not pass away, and his kingdom is one that will never be destroyed. (Daniel 7:13-14)

In John's revelation, he sees a similar scene as well:

Then I saw in the right hand of him who sat on the throne a scroll with writing on both sides and sealed with seven seals. And I saw a mighty angel proclaiming in a loud voice, "Who is worthy to break the seals and open the scroll?" But no one in heaven or on earth or under the earth could open the scroll or even look inside it. I wept and wept because no one was found who was worthy to open the scroll or look inside. Then one of the elders said to me, "Do not weep! See, the Lion of the tribe of Judah, the Root of David, has triumphed. He is able to open the scroll and its seven seals."

Then I saw a Lamb, looking as if it had been slain, standing at the center of the throne, encircled by the four living creatures and the elders. The Lamb had seven horns and seven eyes, which are the seven spirits of God sent out into all the earth. He went and took the scroll from the right hand of him who sat on the throne. And when he had taken it, the four living creatures and the twenty-four elders fell down before the Lamb. Each one had a harp and they were holding golden bowls full of incense, which are the prayers of God's people. And they sang a new song, saying: "You are worthy to take the scroll and to open its seals, because you were slain, and with your blood you purchased for God persons from every tribe and language and people and nation. You have made them to be a kingdom and priests to serve our God, and they will reign on the earth." (Revelation 5:1-10)

Some early Church commentators interpreted the scroll with writing on each side as the Old and New Testaments. Christ alone can break open the truth of all scripture because He is the author and fulfillment of the scriptures. None of the first commentators wrote that this scene from the Revelation was the literal ascension entrance of Jesus, but the scene certainly speaks of the evidence of that ascension to glory. The triumphant Lamb, by the worthiness of His death and resurrection, begins to exercise His authority from Heaven's Throne through the global Church. The ascension of Jesus to the Throne of Heaven births the Messianic Kingdom and the Church Age.

Though Premillennialists believe a restoration of Israel into the Kingdom is ahead of us, that in no way should weaken the complete sovereignty with which Jesus leads His Bridal People now.

Returning To My Dad's House

I began this chapter with the scene of watching thunder storms on our parsonage porch as a kid. In the summer of 2008, I returned to that house. It was a beautiful Sunday afternoon. My Dad's old Methodist Church across the street was still a vibrant congregation. I chuckled as I saw the sermon title for that morning. "There's a Storm A-Coming!"

To be warned is a form of love. The purpose of End Time prophecy is to prepare the Bridal People and warn the Earth that Jesus is coming soon. Since I believe that a time of Great Tribulation prophesied by Jesus will precede His return and that return could be in my generation, I am compelled in love to prepare everyone I can. A storm warning may be unsettling, but better to be prepared than surprised.

People who see very hard times ahead are often stereotyped as depressing to be around or disengaged from trying to make this present world a better place. The greatest trials *are* still ahead. But so is the greatest triumph! The Gospel story doesn't end on the day of Jesus' crucifixion. There is resurrection on Sunday morning. There is life after death. There is the Carpenter from Nazareth sitting on Heaven's Throne! There is solid hope for a better and very real future history. Any truly Christian view of the future must be full of faith, hope, and love for those who trust the leadership of Jesus.

Chapter 6

Toward the Global Finish Line

"You who call upon the Lord, give yourselves no rest,
and give Him no rest till He establishes Jerusalem
and makes her the praise of the earth."
(Isaiah 62:6-7)

Progressive Revelation

Not everyone who loves and follows Jesus has a strong belief about the end of history. Many actively resist the whole subject and believe it displeases God to study it in depth. "Why should we live any differently from any other generation? Didn't Jesus say that we wouldn't know the day or the hour of His coming?"

Jesus told those living in His day it was not given to *them* to know the time of the Kingdom's arrival. But He did not say that future generations would not know at least the season of such an important event. The reason He gave signs and predictions was that future generations *would* know their place in the human story. Much of both Old and New Testaments describe the conditions in the Earth that will apply directly only to the last generation alive at His return.

When God was about to bring the flood in Noah's generation to cleanse the Earth of the defilement from many wicked generations, He gave the world more than a century of warning through Noah's building of a big boat and Noah's preaching of coming judgment.

Noah didn't know the day that the rains would start when he *began* building the ark, but God did tell him the day one week before the first drops:

"Seven days from now I will send rain on the Earth for forty days and forty nights, and I will wipe from the face of the Earth every living creature I have made. . . And after the seven days the floodwaters came on the Earth." (Genesis 7:4, 10)

God doesn't withhold vital information from His friends as the time of massive events draw near. This principle is stated in Amos 3:7: "Surely the Sovereign Lord does *nothing* without revealing His plan to His servants the prophets."

When God was about to bring fire from Heaven down on the wicked cities of Sodom and Gomorrah He did not withhold what He was planning from His friend Abraham. He wanted Abraham to "bargain" with Him for mercy. God *delights* to show mercy. He wants His friends to talk Him *out* of pouring out His anger! That is what God's Son was doing on the Jerusalem Cross for you and me. Inviting us into intercession for mercy is one of the ways that we learn the depth of who Yahweh is. By participating with Him in His heart and plans we learn His emotions and His value system. He wants us to live in the same tension and stress as those with whom we share real time in order that we would compassionately call our generation to receive God's mercy right up until the time the door is closed.

However, the door *will* close. The storms of water and fire from the past warn us still that God is not going to put up with human rebellion and foolishness forever. The Earth is being defiled as I write and the anger of God against the wicked leaders of the planet and those who follow them today is mounting with every hardened heart. Our generation is storing up wrath for a perfect storm on the horizon.

For nearly two thousand years the warning to take refuge from coming judgment of Jesus has been preached. Jesus said, "And this Gospel of the Kingdom will be preached to all nations as a testimony to all people and then the end will come" (Matthew 24:14).

God is not planning a sneak attack. The news of Jesus coming again isn't even news to many people in our post-Christian, Western culture anymore. We have gotten over the idea that a direct future confrontation with the God of the Universe is our biggest problem.

The Good News of the Kingdom Come *and* Coming

The Gospel, or "good news" of the Kingdom, is two-fold and all who know Jesus must know and preach both parts. The good news of mercy and forgiveness at the cross has never lost its luster! We truly can get lost in the amazing grace of God displayed in His willingness to cause His own dear Son to take the punishment for our weakness and rebellion upon Himself. We have *nothing* without the cross! We will never tire of its majestic revelation even throughout eternity.

The resurrected body of Jesus still had the marks of His beating, whipping, and crucifixion when He came to His disciples. Thomas got invited to put his hands in the glorified wounds of Jesus. There were a lot of wounds to choose from. We will always be reminded of the terrible price our Savior paid for loving us when we gaze on Him through endless Ages. I wonder if that is part of what grips the hearts of those twenty-four elders John met in his Throne Room visit recorded in the book of Revelation. Those elders constantly gaze on Him around His Throne and fall down with every glimpse. Those beautiful wounds in Jesus' body never let us forget the depth of His commitment to us.

This image is described in verse 2 of the classic hymn, "Crown Him with Many Crowns."

Crown Him the Lord of Love, behold His hands and side,
Rich wounds yet visible above, in beauty glorified.
No angel in the sky, can fully bear that sight
But downward bends his wondering eye at mysteries so bright.

(The Hymnal for Worship and Celebration, Word Music, Waco, TX, 1986, hymn #234, text by Matthew Bridges)

There Will Be Blood!

The passion and cross of Jesus is glorious, but it is not the *end* of the story. The body of Jesus spattered in His own blood at Golgotha near the gate of Jerusalem covers the blood guilt of all who surrender to Him as their Bridegroom King. But here comes the unpleasant part. The blood of all those who do not receive His Kingdom will stain His body when He returns. Listen to this prophetic picture of the Messiah given by Isaiah in Chapter 63:1-4:

"Who is this coming from Edom, from Bozrah, with his garments stained crimson? Who is this robed in splendor, striding forward in the greatness of his strength?"

"It is I, speaking in righteousness, mighty to save."

"Why are your garments red, like those of one treading the winepress?"

"I have trodden the winepress alone; from the nations no one was with me. I trampled them in my anger and trod them down in my wrath; their blood spattered my garments, and I stained all my clothing. For the day of vengeance was in my heart, and the year of my redemption has come."

Don't get in the way of God and His people. He is coming for them and the blood of those who have mistreated God's people through the ages will run deep.

Many churches have beautiful stained glass windows with Jesus as a gentle shepherd carrying a little lamb on His shoulders. I have yet to see a stained glass window showing this image of Jesus from Isaiah 63 or Revelation 19:11-18 which is its companion passage in the New Testament.

I saw Heaven standing open and there before me was a white horse, whose rider is called Faithful and True. With justice He judges and makes war. His eyes are like blazing fire, and on His head are many crowns. He has a name written on Him that no one knows but He Himself. He is dressed in a robe dipped in blood, and His name is the Word of God. The armies of Heaven were following Him, riding on white horses and dressed in fine linen, white and clean. Out of His mouth comes a sharp sword with which to strike down the nations. "He will rule them with an iron scepter." He treads the winepress of the fury of the wrath of God Almighty. On His robe and on His thigh He has this name written: KING OF KINGS AND LORD OF LORDS.

And I saw an angel standing in the sun, who cried in a loud voice to all the birds flying in midair, "Come, gather together for the great supper of God, so that you may eat the flesh of kings, generals, and mighty men, of horses and their riders, and the flesh of all people, free and slave, small and great."

The Jesus of Bethlehem is also the Jesus of Armageddon. The news of God's Kingdom is mercy to the world. But the terms of citizenship are total surrender to King Jesus. When He returns many who have not already died in terrible judgments will die in His supernatural conquest over the resistance to His leadership.

Though many in the Western World are deaf to the warnings coming from Heaven through the Bridal People, other peoples and cultures are hearing this news. "Get ready! Change your allegiances! The Kingdom of God is near!" This message is still circling the globe. Africa, South America, Asia, and the islands of the Earth are hearing and receiving the good news of Jesus at an astounding rate. The number of people whose cultures don't have lovers of Jesus is getting smaller very quickly. Never in human history have we been so close to fulfilling Jesus' mandate to make citizen-priests of His Kingdom from every nation, tribe, and tongue.

The Global Racetrack

When Peter preached his first sermon in the streets of Jerusalem it was like a starter's gun going off for a track race. For the most part, the historical movement of those cultures that embraced the message of Jesus and bowed to His Lordship went North and West from the Middle East. As the Gospel of the Kingdom spread from Europe to the New World it went throughout the Western Hemisphere. In the last couple of centuries the continents of Africa, Australia, and Asia have seen remarkable growth in the world Christian movement.

The Chinese house-churches consist of over 100 million people. Since the 1920's some of their leaders have had a vision they call the "Back to Jerusalem" movement. They recognize they are 11th hour workers like Jesus talked about in a parable in Mathew chapter 20. They are hired late in terms of the fact that it has only been in the last century that so many Asian believers are being mustered for the task of world evangelism. But they are rejoicing that some of the toughest remaining turf on the planet is "left" for them.

Perhaps no other nation is a better example of speedy movement from other beliefs into the global Christian community than the South Koreans. The missionary zeal of the Korean Church is a huge reason why the ground has been broken across many of the hardest to reach areas of the Earth. The evangelical Church in Korea has only existed for little more than 100 years!

The regions between the Far East and the Middle East (including North Africa) represent the heart of Islam, Buddhism, and Hinduism. It is through these lands that trade routes called the "Silk Road" first linked societies in Europe and East Asia by caravans and shipping. Now it is the Gospel of Jesus Christ that is passing through desert villages in Afghanistan and Iran, high mountain passes in the Pamirs and Himalayas, and seaports from Shanghai to Morrocco back to Jerusalem.

It has been my family's privilege to help birth a Christian student movement in the heart of a Muslim Central Asian Nation. God is at work in parts of Eurasia that have not had numerous followers of Jesus for many centuries since the Nestorian Christian movement was wiped out in the 1400's under the devastating empire of Tamerlane. (Dickens, Nestorian Christianity in Central Asia, 18)

On a recent trip through Central Asia and the Arabian Peninsula, I witnessed many baptisms, prayed with young Arab and Persian followers of Jesus from Muslim backgrounds and heard of stories of many more hearts turning to Jesus behind the veil of Islam. The testimonies of Hindu, Buddhist, and Muslim people placing their faith in Jesus in areas of the world where it could cost them their lives are too sensitive to print here. But it is a dramatic underground movement gaining momentum as you read this chapter.

Since 1985, I have been praying for a house of prayer to be planted in Mecca in Saudi Arabia. Why pray for a city in the Earth where it is unlawful for anyone who is not a Muslim to enter? Why not?

Every inch of this planet and every heart that beats on it is the object of Jesus' love. I believe that before His return there will be a great harvest of those who learn to trust Jesus in the very heartlands of non-Christian cultures. Most of the growth will come not from the sacrifices of Western missionaries, but from the bold witness of new believers among the people themselves. Martyrdom will be a significant part of the price of seeing hard hearts turn to Jesus.

Nothing less than this is the inheritance of Jesus and the destiny of the Saints described in Revelation 7:9: "After this I looked and behold, I saw a great number which no one could number of all nations, tribes, peoples, and tongues, standing before the Throne and before the Lamb. . ."

We are rounding the last turn in the global racetrack!

The historical and geographical stage is being set for the final scenario of confrontations laid out in the primary prophetic books of the Bible; the Psalms, Isaiah, Daniel, Ezekiel, Jesus' own predictions in the Gospels concerning the end of the Age, and the Book of Revelation. Jerusalem is indeed the epicenter of the world. Jerusalem was the starting line for the expansion of Jesus' Kingdom. It will be the finish line as well.

The physical descendents of Abraham, Isaac, and Jacob that remain after the final season of great suffering will be saved as they welcome Jesus as their true Messiah to Jerusalem.

God is Gathering a Jewish Welcoming Committee in Jerusalem

Observable conditions are taking place in our generation that Jesus said would be present in the season of His return. Completing the task of preaching the Gospel to every people group on Earth is one of the End Time "mega-signs". Another mega-sign is the Jewish people in Jerusalem who will welcome Him back as the long awaited heir to David's Throne. "You will not see me again until you say, 'Blessed is He that comes in the Name of the Lord'" (Matthew 23:39).

Along with the Back to Jerusalem vision there is another emphasis in the church today called the "Road to Jerusalem." "R2J" is a call to reconcile the Jewish and Gentile followers of Jesus as we draw nearer to His return. Jesus' death on the cross opened the door for all nations to be welcomed as fellow citizens with Israel under the leadership of the Messiah. But even though all of the New Testament authors except Luke were Jewish, and the first disciples were mostly Jewish, things began to change pretty quickly.

As the number of Jewish followers of Jesus grew and non-Jews also began to follow Him in increasing numbers, Messianic Jews were kicked out of synagogues all over the Roman Empire. The early practice of Jesus' followers was to gather on Shabbat (Saturday) at the synagogue. But by the time the apostle John was writing the book of Revelation in circa 90 A.D., he refers to the Lord's Day (Sunday) which was becoming the day when believers were now gathering by necessity.

I John, your brother and companion in the suffering and kingdom and patient endurance that are ours in Jesus, was on the island of Patmos because of the word of God and the testimony of Jesus. On the Lord's Day I was in the Spirit. . . (Rev. 1:9-10)

One of the greatest challenges for the Church in the first 100 years was how to walk out the One New Man reality of Jew and Gentile living in one New Covenant family. Whole books of the New Testament like Romans, Galatians, Acts, and others were written in an attempt to keep Jewish and Gentile disciples relating well across deep cultural divides. Ethnic pride and cultural differences are still some of the greatest barriers toward fulfilling God's dream of a Global Beloved Community.

As the churches in the first century became increasingly Gentile in number and in culture, much of Christianity lost its Jewish flavor and tradition. Later, Gentile communities began to persecute the Jews who were now scattered over the world in minority communities. Too often, this bigotry was done using the name of Jesus. We now look back over many centuries of tragic stories of anti-Semitic crimes initiated or tolerated by Christian communities.

The Jewish holocaust in Germany was a culmination of unredeemed attitudes sown by leaders including Church Reformer Martin Luther centuries earlier.

In spite of so much pain and hardness of heart, Jews today are beginning to sense a genuine support and love coming from Gentile followers of Jesus who are repenting of their arrogance and hatred toward Abraham's physical descendents. Many Jews have discovered for themselves that their Scriptures prophesy of Jesus as Messiah in a way that they have been discouraged by their Rabbis for centuries to consider. Since 1890, when Joseph Rabinowitz opened the first Messianic Jewish synagogue in Moldova, the number of Jews around the world becoming followers of Messiah Jesus is growing at a pace not seen since He walked in Galilee!

Are there still issues that divide Messianic Jews from their Gentile brothers? Yes. How important is keeping Shabbat on Saturday? How important are the Jewish feasts, some of which God commanded they should keep forever? Are Gentile believers required to keep any of these practices as well?

These are emotional issues even amongst Messianic Jewish congregations. Jews laugh at themselves by saying that if you have three Jews in a discussion you will have four opinions!

What is essential is that we respect one another's convictions even as we contend for unity across the global Body of Christ. Gentile believers have MUCH to learn from how Messianic Jews are living out of their Jewish understanding of the Scripture. Can Messianic believers enthusiastically practice Jewish customs without allowing them to become a barrier for brotherhood with others? Will Messianic Israeli believers and Palestinian Arab believers stand together in witness to Jesus in the cross fire of rabbinical Judaism and Islamic zeal?

There is a strong biblical case for keeping the Shabbat, but does it have to be on Saturday? Followers of Jesus in Muslim countries (i.e. the United Arab Emirates) are forced to worship on Friday morning because that is the Islamic weekend. What do we do with scriptures like Colossians 2:17? ("So let no one judge you in food or in drink, or regarding a festival or Sabbaths, which are a shadow of things to come, but the substance is of Christ.")

In this verse Rabbi Paul makes Jewish and Roman dietary laws, festivals, and Sabbaths secondary to becoming a new community of Spirit and Truth. He was convinced that non-Jewish cultural expressions of worship to God were also valid and should be allowed freedom to form dynamically and multiply as long as they were ramps and not barriers to true fellowship with Jesus.

There are no easy practical answers, but I admire the growing global community of Messianic Jewish believers who are ostracized by other Jews and misunderstood by a majority of Gentile Christians. We all need to be humble and teachable as the Day of our Lord draws near. Israel and Jerusalem will only become more central to how our global history will climax.

As we move toward the global finish line, there are still major conditions to be met from a Premillennialist perspective. Specifically, there is currently no temple in Jerusalem that a future political leader could defile. Jesus is coming, but if an Anti-Christ ruler and Third Temple are preceding conditions, we have a while to wait.

Until then, I believe believe the exhortation of Isaiah 62:7 is still for today. "Give Him no rest till He establishes Jerusalem and makes her the praise of the earth." Let's pray continually for more revelation and fulfillment of the prophetic promises of Scripture until Jesus returns and establishes Jerusalem as the City of the Great King!

Chapter 7

The Promise of the Messianic Kingdom

"I have installed My King on Zion, my holy hill."
(Psalm 2:6)

Discerning the Real Leadership of Jesus

Old Testament prophecies of the coming Messiah were bound up with the concepts of justice, righteousness, and shalom. If the foundation of God's government is justice, righteousness, and truth then the King will BE the fullness of those attributes Himself.

In love a Throne will be established, in faithfulness a man will sit on it, one from the House of David, one who in judging seeks justice and speeds the cause of righteousness. (Isaiah 16:15)

Here is my Servant, whom I uphold, my Chosen One in whom I delight; I will put my Spirit on Him and He will bring justice to the nations. He will not shout or cry out, or raise His voice in the streets. A bruised reed He will not break, and a smoldering wick He will not snuff out. In faithfulness He will bring forth justice; He will not falter or be discouraged till He establishes justice on Earth. (Isaiah 42:1-4)

The Original Promise Keeper

When God makes a promise, it doesn't matter how much time goes by before He honors it. He has timetables. But have you noticed how different they seem to be from ours?

There are some serious promises that God made to human beings in the Bible. One of the clearest and most often repeated is His promise to David that one of his sons would govern a real earthly political Kingdom that would last forever. Listen to how strong the language of covenant promise is in God's voice on this matter in just a few places.

God's promise to David first comes through Nathan the prophet in 1 Chronicles 17:10-14:

I declare to you that the LORD will build a house for you: When your days are over and you go to be with your fathers, I will raise up your offspring to succeed you, one of your own sons, and I will establish his kingdom. He is the one who will build a house for me, and I will establish his throne forever. I will be his father, and he will be my son. I will never take my love away from him, as I took it away from your predecessor. I will set him over my house and my kingdom forever; his throne will be established forever.

In a few sentences the word "forever" is repeated three times. Isaiah the prophet picks up the theme of David's messianic successor long after David's immediate successor son, King Solomon, has died.

"I will make an everlasting covenant with you, my faithful love promised to David. See, I have made him a witness to the peoples, a leader and commander of the peoples" (Isaiah 55:3-4).

In the next generation, the prophet Jeremiah picks up where Isaiah left off:

"The days are coming," declares the LORD, "when I will fulfill the gracious promise I made to the house of Israel and to the house of Judah.

"In those days and at that time I will make a righteous Branch sprout from David's line; He will do what is just and right in the land. In those days Judah will be saved and Jerusalem will live in safety. This is the name by which it will be called: 'The LORD Our Righteousness.'

For this is what the LORD says: "David will never fail to have a man to sit on the throne of the house of Israel, nor will the priests, who are Levites, ever fail to have a man to stand before me continually to offer burnt offerings, to burn grain offerings and to present sacrifices."

The word of the LORD came to Jeremiah: "This is what the LORD says: 'If you can break my covenant with the day and my covenant with the night, so that day and night no longer come at their appointed time, then my covenant with David my servant — and my covenant with the Levites who are priests ministering before me — can be broken and David will no longer have a descendant to reign on his throne. I will make the descendants of David my servant and the Levites who minister before me as countless as the stars of the sky and as measureless as the sand on the seashore.'" (Jer. 33:14-24)

Promises like these are why the disciples discussed the timing of the Davidic Kingdom with the risen Jesus in Acts, chapter one. Jesus had just fulfilled many Messianic promises as the Son of David and the Great High Priest who gave Himself as the very Passover Lamb of God sacrificed for all sinners; but He did not, at that time, establish a government centered in Jerusalem. For that reason most Jews today still do not believe that Jesus is the promised Son of David.

Strangers Passing Through

When Christianity loses its connection to a future glorious Kingdom it can be easily reduced to social benefit programs, institution building, or self improvement plans. God does offer us a better life now. I am in favor of great institutions. Jesus promised in John 10:10 that He has come so that we might have life and have it in the fullest reality. There are so many wonderful things to celebrate about the Age we live in now. Jesus knew how to enjoy a good party! But we should never allow ourselves to think that abundant life is simply our best life now.

We are not citizens of this world. According to Peter we are strangers passing through. "Since you call on a Father who judges each man's work impartially, live your lives as *strangers* here in reverent fear" (1 Peter 1:17).

To forget that this Age is not our final destination is to risk losing our soul. Jesus said, "Do not worry about your life, what you will eat or drink; or about your body, what you will wear. Is not life more important than food, and the body more important than clothes? But seek first his kingdom and his righteousness, and all these things will be given to you as well." (Matt. 6:25, 33). Jesus wasn't just admonishing us to have a certain positive outlook on life, though that is a real by-product. He was inviting all with ears to hear to become citizens of a future Kingdom by living its values now.

The Great Hope of the First Generation of Jesus Lovers

But our citizenship is in heaven. And we eagerly await a Savior from there, the Lord Jesus Christ, who by the power that enables Him to bring everything under His control, will transform our lowly bodies so they will be like His glorious body. (Phil. 3:20-21)

The expectation of Jesus' return was foundational to the understanding and motivation of the early Church. The hope of Jesus' return, based on their face to face conversations with Him after His resurrection, fueled *astronomical* courage and endurance for the first generation of Jesus' messengers. We need that kind of solid faith today like nothing else.

The first believers were not bent on creating institutions because they had tasted the Millennial Kingdom and would not settle for less. They wanted to see their Friend and Master running the planet, and expected He would, soon.

Future generations of Christians began to imagine a world where Jesus probably would *not* be returning in their lifetime. We hunkered down. The age of institutionalized (and nominal) religion ripened under the Byzantine Emperor Constantine in 313 A.D. On a global level, Christians have been trying to reconnect to the fullness of the revelation fire and love of the first church ever since. A growing people-movement requires organization. Government is a gift. However, without renewal, cold institutions are what are left after the fires of Heaven's zeal have burned out in human hearts.

My desire is for God to restore the biblical hope and vision of the Millennial Kingdom held in the early Church to our hearts. Why? Because, we miss the real dynamic of "Christianity" when we fail to appreciate the historical context and Spirit of revelation in which it was birthed. To become a follower of Jesus meant putting your life and reputation on the line. Being associated with His name usually put you under horrible social pressure from every side. The first generation of preachers had NO HOPE for a nice vocational ministerial career with a denominational pension plan. But what they *did* have was so much better than what you and I have today.

My generation has been told that God loves us and has a wonderful plan for our lives. That is true. But that wonderful plan is to die to ourselves, be hated by all who hate Jesus' leadership, and live as strangers in this Age before we rule with Him in the next one.

I am not writing about this subject as if I already possess what I am trying to convince you of. I am *just* as vulnerable to the impulse to build my "kingdom" and act like it is the same one Jesus preached in His Sermon from the Mount. We together must *cry out* for the understanding that we do NOT have. Heaven is a real place. We have nothing on Earth unless it is given to us from God.

I think Jesus has me writing this book so that *I* can finish well! If it helps you too, great! But what I understand about God, the Bible, and my own heart is that we are drunk with the delusional culture of this Age. What the world needs from the followers of Jesus is a revolution of revelation from Heaven. We need to be woken up from a sleep of death so we can awaken others. But so many of our Sunday morning gatherings that we equate with "church" just keep the bar open on the cultural cruise ship that is heading into the perfect storm.

You and I need the same first love and certain hope the first Jewish Christians knew. For them, living beyond a martyr's death was more than a theory. It was the example of their Friend. It was the norm. I want our generation to know this hope again. . .in our *guts*. I believe we MUST have it to finish history well as true followers of Jesus. If what Jesus predicted about His followers being hated because of Him and His value system is increasingly true for us or our kids, then you and I cannot keep moving forward without a compelling vision of a planetary life bigger than this one.

What If We Preached the Millennial Kingdom to our Kids?

Caleb, my amazing middle son, graduated from a public high school in one of the most prosperous counties in our Bible Belt region. But even with all the youth groups and churches in our area, many of his friends were giving themselves to X-rated versions of Disney's High School Musical movies. Drugs, sex, narcissism, elite lifestyles, yada, yada. Watching my son's peer group was a reality check.

But what if they knew what gripped the hearts of Jesus' youth group, a.k.a. the disciples? Being around Jesus and His friends put you closest to the most intensely pleasurable, adventuresome life possible! What if Caleb's friends knew that the fun lasted longer than one night stands? What if they knew that the Kingdom Jesus is bringing with His friends is a grander adventure than any Bruckheimer film? The intrigue of that adventure is what caused Peter, James, and John to quit their jobs just to be around this Jesus guy.

It is hard to blame our kids and our culture of thinking that the Kingdom of God is boring when our "church life" seems that way compared to beer commercials, reality TV, or tabloid magazines. Maybe if they were convinced of something far better to live for they would decide to leave the tragic counterfeit life styles that are eating their souls alive.

The vision of persevering with courage and faith through a world of opposition in order to rule and reign with Jesus in a dynamic future is the inheritance of *every* disciple. It is part of Christianity 101, not 301. A life of real time partnership with Jesus now in order to receive "super-bodies" in the Age to Come ought to be highly motivating for us all. I am seriously looking forward to it! Move over X-Men! The Bible's view of an incredible future helps us to live without compromising with the dark powers of this Age.

In many churches today the very heart throb of the first Christians, the Millennial Kingdom, is rarely preached. Most people's idea of the future preached by Christians is some bland notion of walking through clouds strumming on a harp and singing for eons. I believe the Bible gives us plenty of reasons to believe that the future Jesus brings is literally Heaven on Earth.

If only for this life we have hope in Christ, we are to be pitied more than all men. But Christ has indeed been raised from the dead. . .so in Christ all will be made alive. But each in his own turn: Christ, the firstfruits; then when He comes, those who belong to Him. Then the end will come, when He hands over the Kingdom to God the Father after He has destroyed all dominion, authority and power. For He must reign until He has put all His enemies under His feet. (1 Cor 15:19-25)

Restoring the Eschatology of the Apostles

This passage, written by Paul, carries the implication of a Millennial Kingdom laid out in the sequence of Revelation 19 through 22. (1 - The Return of Jesus, 2 - The Millennial Kingdom, 3 – The Final Judgment, and 4 – The New Heaven and New Earth.) Because it is not a more explicit passage concerning a visible earthly kingdom, those who are not convinced of a literal Millennial period, are not swayed. However, one can argue that the eschatology of Paul as a good Jewish rabbi *assumed* a future earthly Kingdom with Jerusalem as its capital. The plausibility of the first generation of Jesus' followers having a consensus expectation for a Davidic Kingdom to be set up at Jesus' return, may be a reason why there is not a great deal of detail about it as the scriptures formed.

Many of the New Testament Apostles' letters were written to correct competing beliefs in the newly forming churches. The idea that there *were no* competing eschatological views to a future Davidic government in that first generation may explain why little is written.

There may simply have been no strong alternate eschatology to correct at that time.

Theologians who argue for positions different from the eschatology of the Jews of the later Old Testament period or the Apostles who wrote the New Testament (both of which, I believe, assumed an earthly Davidic government from Jerusalem) need to recognize that they are making assumptions about eschatology based on theological developments more than one hundred years after most of the Bible was written. Amillennial and Postmillennial views are at risk of reinterpreting the eschatology of the apostolic church and of Jesus Himself.

Papias, an early church father, lived from 70-155. He knew Polycarp and John, the author of Revelation, and others who had seen the Lord. Papias' original works are lost, but fragments of his words are preserved in the quotations of later Church Fathers.

Eusebius writes about Papias saying, ". . .he says that there will be a millennium after the resurrection from the dead, when the personal reign of Christ will be established on this earth" (*Hist. Eccl. 3. 39*).

Only a few early Church Fathers wrote about the Millennium. But most of those who wrote before 250 A.D. viewed the Millennium to be future and literal as opposed to present and symbolic. Writers of this period believed the Millennium of Revelation 20 to be a time *designed for post-resurrected believers*, not pre-resurrected believers.

In any case, the sequence of the Return of Jesus, the Millennial Kingdom, the Final Judgment, and New Heaven and New Earth, is consistent within the revelation of the Bible. Holding to this sequence clears up many areas of theological dissonance confusing millions today. I believe that as the Premillennialism of the Apostles is restored in the coming decades, courage and hope will sky rocket in the people of God once again. This concrete view of Jesus returning to keep every promise made by God to men, including those made to ethnic descendants of Abraham, will be the fuel enabling Jesus' lovers to lay down their lives during a generation that will hate His leadership.

The passion of God in the first two chapters of the Bible in Genesis is to dwell with Man in visible partnership on the Earth! The passion of God in the last two chapters of the Bible in Revelation is to dwell with Man in visible partnership on the Earth! God is keeping a promise not only to us, but to Himself. These are the biblical bookends of human history. At the end of the Millennial Kingdom Jesus destroys all opposition to His leadership and the Father comes with the Holy City in a New Heaven and New Earth.

I saw the Holy City, the New Jerusalem, coming down out of heaven from God, prepared as a bride beautifully dressed for her husband. And I heard a loud voice from the throne saying, "Now the dwelling of God is with men, and he will live with them. They will be his people, and God himself will be with them and be their God. He will wipe every tear from their eyes. There will be no more death or mourning or crying or pain, for the old order of things has passed away." (Rev. 22:2-4)

The greatest promise is still ahead.

Chapter 8

Motivated By Joy

"Let us fix our eyes on Jesus, the author and finisher of our faith,
who for the joy set before Him endured the cross, scorning its
shame, and sat down at the right hand of the throne of God.
Consider Him who endured such opposition from sinful men,
so that you will not grow weary and lose heart."
(Hebrews 12:2-3)

The Best is Yet to Come

An eternal community of "Voluntary Lovers" that celebrate Jesus and partner with Him in ruling the universe is the dream of God that compels Him to act in each of our lives and in history the way He does. John saw this vision of Heaven in Revelation Chapter 7. It is our joyful destiny!

After this I looked and there before me was a great multitude that no one could count, from every nation, tribe, people and language, standing before the throne and in front of the Lamb. They were wearing white robes and were holding palm branches in their hands. And they cried out in a loud voice: "Salvation belongs to our God, who sits on the throne, and to the Lamb."

All the angels were standing around the throne and around the elders and the four living creatures. They fell down on their faces before the throne and worshiped God, saying:

"Amen! Praise and glory and wisdom and thanks and honor and power and strength be to our God forever and ever. Amen!"

Then one of the elders asked me, "These in white robes—who are they, and where did they come from?" I answered, "Sir, you know."

And he said, "These are they who have come out of the great tribulation; they have washed their robes and made them white in the blood of the Lamb. Therefore, they are before the throne of God and serve him day and night in his temple; and he who sits on the throne will spread his tent over them. Never again will they hunger; never again will they thirst. The sun will not beat upon them, nor any scorching heat. For the Lamb at the center of the throne will be their shepherd; he will lead them to springs of living water. And God will wipe away every tear from their eyes. (Rev 7:9-17)

In God's Throne Room, there are dazzling sights, sounds, aromas, shakings, conversations, pregnant pauses, crescendos, emotions, and on and on if you read the whole Revelation. God's Majestic creativity on display! God doesn't want us to get stuck on the scary and painful stuff of life. Righteousness, peace, and joy in the Holy Spirit, that's the Kingdom of God. Dialoging with the Holy Spirit and worshipping God through Him keeps the hope and beauty of God's presence real in our hearts until we see Him on His Throne with our very own glorified eyes. Until then, every child of God bears a cross of suffering. Jesus is our great example of how to carry it.

Let us fix our eyes on Jesus, the author and finisher of our faith, who for the joy set before Him endured the cross, scorning its shame, and sat down at the right hand of the throne of God. Consider Him who endured such opposition from sinful men, so that you will not grow weary and lose heart. (Hebrews 12:2-3)

It is for JOY that Jesus endured great suffering. It is for JOY that all those who know Him also endure great suffering. Are we convinced about spending eternity with Jesus in a glorious future? Do we have a joyful vision of a future with Him that will keep our love from growing cold during the rising tide of global evil? Are we married to this present Age? Or are we exercising the "present value" of the blood of Jesus to live wisely by working and waiting for the Age to come?

Most busy days, we may not even give our eternal future a passing thought. That is the reality of my life sometimes. But I am not content to settle in that state. If we lose our hope of Heaven being reunited with Earth, we will end up living to the beat of the Spirit of this Age; and lose our soul. Jesus told us to "always pray and not give up" (Luke 18:1)! Prayer is what keeps us awake to His coming. Constant prayer is how we stay in agreement with His vision, values, and plans and not our own.

The Throne Room Vision of John

In the Revelation given to him by Jesus, the beloved disciple John does his best to encourage the seven churches in Asia Minor (and vicariously to subsequent readers) to persevere through intense suffering by describing these things he saw in a vision:

1) The resurrected Jesus in His glory.
2) The rewards when Jesus' people stay on track and consequences when they blow it.
3) The glorious dynamism of the Throne Room of God.
4) How those who trust in Jesus' leadership participate in His triumph over every cosmic contender.
5) How God keeps His promise to bring the Messianic Kingdom in Heaven to Earth for a thousand year period under the visible leadership of Jesus.
6) The triumphal procession of the Bride of Jesus through all Ages descending as the Heavenly Jerusalem.

The Revelation given to John is a vision that has stirred the holy imagination and provided joyful motivation for Bridal People throughout the centuries. Jesus may look like a loser to the skeptical world now, but just you wait! He is "Da Winnamon!" That is Jamaican English for "you WANT to be on this Guy's team!"

Any reader of the Revelation given to John has to decide at some point if his report is all mere symbolism or if it is a poetic description of literal realities. John uses gem stones to describe the brilliance of the Heavenly City. The detail of the lists of precious stones and metals is either a sign of his sanctified imagination gone wild or he is reporting a very literal scene using lots of poetic description when only a few details would have done as well. I am going to err on the literal side. If John didn't see something REAL, then what is the difference between the book of Revelation and a hallucination?

Is there symbolic language in John's writings? Yes. But metaphors don't kick demon butt. An allegory doesn't love you unto death on a cross. Cool ideas and faddish dreams don't stack up to a real Man who was alive, dead, alive again and looks at you with "eyes like a flame of fire" (Rev 1:14). If you read the Revelation as if it were John's creative writing project while killing time on the Island of Patmos, then you can see some cool academic literary devices. But if you read the Revelation as an Eyewitness News Report of the really real and yet to come then you will tremble as John did and fall at Jesus' feet in total worship (Rev. 1:17).

The book of Revelation is largely ignored in the preaching of mainstream Western churches. Why isn't understanding this book being encouraged more in our churches today, especially since the Book of Revelation has a promise and blessing in it (Rev 1:3) for all who read and hear and keep those things written in it? You wouldn't read an exciting thriller of a story and not read the final chapter would you? The Book of Revelation is the last five minutes of the season finale of your favorite TV series. Why would you want to miss that?

There are several reasons why people, Christian and non- Christian alike, are discouraged from reading the Book of Revelation.

1) **"I am not smart enough."** Even though the original book was intended to be read so that the Christians in Asia Minor could receive its blessing, the idea that only scholarly theologians and history professors can ever understand its complex meaning has taken deep root.

2) **"I don't want to become weird."** Though becoming socially awkward may not be a bad thing in itself, some people are afraid of becoming like messengers who communicate the Book of Revelation in an eccentric style, constantly pumping out ever changing credibility numbing scenarios and fantastic predictions based on the latest newspaper headlines or personal experiences.

3) **"The Book of Revelation scares the bejeebers out of me!"** Thinking about the end of the world is depressing and terrifying if not understood in exactly the way Jesus reveals the future to us. There is a popular misconception that the last generation of Christians gets beat up until a remnant is left trembling in a cave contemplating suicide. Then Jesus comes. If that *were* true, it pretty much stinks.

The 66th Book of the Bible is a gift to every follower of Jesus. It is not to be ignored. The Book of Revelation is a vision of how God's Bridal People, leading up to the generation alive when Jesus returns, will triumph over all the visible and invisible fallen world can throw at us.

Perhaps no one today is doing more to energize young adults with a passion for Jesus and the relevance of biblical prophecy than Mike Bickle. The International House of Prayer community founded by him in Kansas City is constantly gazing on the beauty of Jesus and His word to be faithful signposts in the climactic days ahead. Mike calls the Book of Revelation a prayer manual and battle plan for the triumphant church. For him it is the Book of Exodus and the Book of Acts converging in the last generation before the Millennial Kingdom is established.

The degree of futurism and literalism in Mike's way of reading the language of Revelation will not resonate with everyone, but no one can accuse Mike Bickle of not taking scripture seriously.

I believe that if we are to be prepared for the leadership of Jesus when He returns we must digest the vision of John. The generation alive during the last seven years before Jesus splits the skies will live and breathe it. But, the genius of God's word is that it can speak to any generation. The Revelation was highly motivating to John's generation which was being fed to lions and marginalized in every city. They had glory, wealth, life, and unspeakable joy to look forward to in the presence of God Himself! They would inherit this restored planet in spite of the fact that wicked leaders looked fully in charge. Every generation of Jesus-lovers needs this reality burning in their heart to stay fully alive.

Even if we punt the whole discussion of literal or symbolic readings of Revelation, we still have the plain teaching of Jesus in the gospel narratives declaring how He will come with God's glory leading angel armies to establish His leadership on earth with those not ashamed of Him:

Then (Jesus) called the crowd to him along with his disciples and said: "If anyone would come after me, he must deny himself and take up his cross and follow me. For whoever wants to save his life will lose it, but whoever loses his life for me and for the gospel will save it. What good is it for a man to gain the whole world, yet forfeit his soul? Or what can a man give in exchange for his soul? If anyone is ashamed of me and my words in this adulterous and sinful generation, the Son of Man will be ashamed of him when he comes in his Father's glory with the holy angels. (Mark 8:34-38)

Following the leadership of Jesus is a call to die to this passing Age, but the pleasures of the Age He is bringing far surpass pleasures now. Our glad God motivates with joy! He has given us the revelation of the Throne Room and the promise of a glorious future through John. Gazing on Jesus strengthens His Bride's heart with love to finish life and history well and fall into His embrace with unspeakable joy!

Chapter 9

The Bridegroom King Is Coming

"Wake up, O sleeper, rise from the dead,
and Christ will shine on you."
(Ephesians 5:14)

Staying Awake or Sleeping the Sleep of Death

Jesus used wedding imagery and likened Himself to a Bridegroom when speaking of His Bridal People during the season of His return. In Matthew 25:1-13, Jesus tells a parable about ten watchful women:

At that time the kingdom of heaven will be like ten virgins who took their lamps and went out to meet the bridegroom. Five of them were foolish and five were wise. The foolish ones took their lamps but did not take any oil with them. The wise, however, took oil in jars along with their lamps. The bridegroom was a long time in coming, and they all became drowsy and fell asleep.

At midnight the cry rang out: 'Here's the bridegroom! Come out to meet him!'

Then all the virgins woke up and trimmed their lamps. The foolish ones said to the wise, 'Give us some of your oil; our lamps are going out.'

'No,' they replied, 'there may not be enough for both us and you. Instead, go to those who sell oil and buy some for yourselves.'

But while they were on their way to buy the oil, the bridegroom arrived. The virgins who were ready went in with him to the wedding banquet. And the door was shut.

Later the others also came. 'Sir! Sir!' they said. 'Open the door for us!'

But he replied, 'I tell you the truth, I don't know you.'

Therefore keep watch, because you do not know the day or the hour.

We do not know the day or hour but Jesus gave many signs of the season in which His return for His Bride would occur. Since Jesus rebuked His generation for not understanding the hour of their visitation and failing to recognize Him as Messiah, is it not reasonable to believe that He expects the last generation to understand their appointed time? Is that not the purpose of His describing the conditions of the Earth when He would keep His promise? He commanded us to "watch and pray" and eagerly anticipate His coming.

He sends warnings and messengers so we will be ready and *not* caught off guard, "like a thief in the night." Do not ignore the signs in our generation and say that today is no different than a thousand years ago. The signs of His return are ripening. The time is growing short and Jesus *wants* His Bridal People to be ready for our Wedding Day.

Going Out to Meet the Bridegroom King

Jesus' death on the cross as an atoning sacrifice saves us from the wrath of God, but His suffering is no guarantee that we won't suffer. In fact, the example of Jesus' sacrificial life is so that we *will* suffer with Him. Therefore, I would not encourage anyone to accept the theory of the pre-tribulation "rapture" made popular through the "Left Behind" novels and many TV preachers.

The Pre-tribulation Rapture theory teaches that the Bride of Jesus will meet Him in the air and go *back* to Heaven with Him for up to seven years while ethnic Israel goes through the great global persecution. The Greek word (αρπάζω), pronounced harpazo and interpreted as "rapture", simply means "caught up." 1 Thessalonians 4:16-17 is the passage that refers to being "caught up" to meet Jesus in the air.

Theologian Dr. George Ladd makes a case in *The Blessed Hope* (91) that the Bride of Jesus meets Him in the air, just as the wise virgins go out to meet the Bridegroom at midnight, to join all the others who are coming with Him on our way back to see Jesus fulfill promises on earth.

The Greek word, "apantesis" (απάντησις) translated as "meet," appears only three undisputed places in the New Testament. The first is in the story we just heard from Jesus of the virgins who go out to meet the Bridegroom on the way to the wedding celebration. The second is in the 1 Thessalonians 4:16-17 passage that is used to support the rapture theory:

For the Lord Himself will come down from heaven, with a loud command, with the voice of the archangel and the trumpet call of God, and the dead in Christ will rise first. After that, we who are still alive and are left will be caught up together with them in the clouds to meet the Lord in the air. And so we will be with the Lord forever.

The third occurrence of apantesis is in Acts 28:15 where the believers in Rome go outside the city to "meet" the apostle Paul on his way into the city.

It is consistent with the cultural understanding of the time to believe that God's people will meet Jesus in the air as He comes back to Earth in glory as a Bridegroom King and Judge to establish God's reign. It will be the best day ever for God's People. It will be the worst day ever for those unprepared to receive the leadership of Jesus.

Heavenly Intimidation

For as lightning that comes from the east is visible even in the west, so will be the coming of the Son of Man.

At that time the sign of the Son of Man will appear in the sky, and all the nations of the earth will mourn. They will see the Son of Man coming on the clouds of the sky, with power and great glory. And He will send his angels with a loud trumpet call, and they will gather His elect from the four winds, from one end of the heavens to the other. (Matt. 24:27, 30-31)

In order for the coming of the Son of Man to be visible to the whole world "just as the lightning comes from the east and flashes into the west" there are a few possibilities to consider. The traditional image of the return of Jesus is a direct vertical descent from out of the dimension of Heaven to Jerusalem. But if every nation will witness this event on something other than Fox News, it makes sense to consider that He will first make many laps around the planet with the armies of Heaven as He gathers His sons and daughters from around the world to meet Him in the air. This will take some time.

This event has a type of predecessor in the Book of Joshua when the city of Jericho was encircled by an invading Israel once a day for six days before the seventh day when they marched seven times around the city. After the last trip around the city, trumpets were blown, Israel shouted, and the walls disintegrated. Up until that moment, the people inside Jericho were paralyzed by fear.

Perhaps that will be the state of people around the world during the return of Jesus. They and the world media will witness with their own eyes hundreds of millions of people and angels circling the planet in the air. The sight of Jesus and countless angels and saints being gathered like an army for a final confrontation will have a chilling effect on the nations and armies of the Earth. This image may sound far-fetched to many readers, since alien invasions popularized in movies have the good guys on the ground; but the return of Jesus will be an invasion from out of Heaven that first appears in our skies. He is not coming alone. He is coming back with His friends. The good guys are the ones in the sky who know that Jesus is the only One with a clear title deed to Planet Earth. The best Pentagon technologies will be no match for angel armies.

David wrote a song nearly four thousand years ago that paints this picture of Divine confrontation with the political systems of the Earth:

Why do the nations conspire and the peoples plot in vain? The kings of the earth take their stand and the rulers gather together against the LORD and against His Anointed One. "Let us break their chains," they say, "and throw off their fetters." The One enthroned in Heaven laughs; the Lord scoffs at them. Then He rebukes them in His anger and terrifies them in His wrath, saying, "I have installed my King on Zion, my holy hill."

I will proclaim the decree of the LORD: He said to me, 'You are my Son; today I have become your Father. Ask of me, and I will make the nations your inheritance, the ends of the earth your possession. You will rule them with an iron scepter; you will dash them to pieces like pottery.' Therefore, you kings, be wise; be warned, you rulers of the earth. Serve the LORD with fear and rejoice with trembling. Kiss the Son, lest He be angry and you be destroyed in your way, for His wrath can flare up in a moment. Blessed are all who take refuge in Him. (Psalm 2)

Jealous For Good Leadership

The LORD their God will save his people on that day as a shepherd saves his flock. They will sparkle in his land like jewels in a crown. (Zech. 9:16)

God is Jealous. Many people are offended by the concept that God's nature includes jealousy. However, His jealousy is not a character flaw to be compared to a petty boyfriend. God has no competition. God is not jealous *of* anyone. God is jealous *for* His own purposes and plans. He grieves that so much of human experience is marked by poor shepherds of His people. Liars, power-mongers, deceivers, murderers, and greedy tyrants have had the leadership of our planet for too long. The best of human institutions are marked by our foibles.

God wants the world to know Him through the greatness of His leadership. He has prepared a King, in His very own Son, to Shepherd the Earth for a thousand years. As the true Messiah, Jesus will model both the depth of meekness and love already shown on the Cross, but also the authority and power to enforce righteousness, justice, and truth in the years ahead. Those who choose Him now will partner with Him then.

Therefore wait for me," declares the LORD, "for the day I will stand up to testify. I have decided to assemble the nations, to gather the kingdoms and to pour out my wrath on them all my fierce anger. The whole world will be consumed by the fire of my jealous anger. Then will I purify the lips of the peoples, that all of them may call on the name of the LORD and serve him shoulder to shoulder. (Zephaniah 3:8,9)

God's jealousy might be better understood as passion and zeal. If jealousy sounds a bit too negative for your ears, zeal rooted in eternal righteousness, justice, and truth is really what the Bible reveals about God:

Of the increase of his government and peace there will be no end. He will reign on David's throne and over his kingdom, establishing and upholding it with justice and righteousness from that time on and forever. The zeal of the LORD Almighty will accomplish this (Is. 9:7)

His zeal is not only for humanity. His zeal is for the real estate of the Earth as well. He made everything good in the beginning and He is longing to finish what He started. Human history as we know it is an interruption of that grand plan due to human sin and Satanic deception. God is committed to correcting every lie and cleaning up every land title deed. His return is about setting everything in the human record straight. In order for that global witness to occur, there must be a Man of God's choosing who will bring the leadership the world has yet to experience He wants all of humanity to see what has been on His mind from the beginning. He will display His glory in the community of those who have put their trust and hope in Him. Those who rejected His love in Jesus will grieve with "gnashing of teeth" the fact of being blind to what was hidden in plain view for Ages in the Bible.

David sang in Psalm 37:10: "A little while and the wicked will be no more, though you look for them, they will not be found. But the meek will inherit the land and enjoy great peace." Jesus picked up the chorus and said in Matthew 5:5: "Blessed are the meek, for they will inherit the Earth."

All the wealth of the world is being stored up for Jesus and His friends to enjoy. The meek will inherit the earth not through political conquest in this Age but through friendship with Earth's coming King. Isaiah describes the glory of Jerusalem in the day it becomes the capital city of the Millennium.

Arise, shine, for your light has come, and the glory of the LORD rises upon you. See, darkness covers the earth and thick darkness is over the peoples, but the LORD rises upon you and his glory appears over you. Nations will come to your light, and kings to the brightness of your dawn. "Lift up your eyes and look about you: All assemble and come to you; your sons come from afar, and your daughters are carried on the arm. Then you will look and be radiant, your heart will throb and swell with joy; the wealth on the seas will be brought to you, to you the riches of the nations will come. (Isaiah 60:1-5)

Confrontations with the rulers who resist Jesus will precede the dawn of rebuilding. God will have His Global King in Zion. His promises to David of a descendant who will always lead God's people as a Good Shepherd will be kept. But while we are looking up for our Bridegroom King to come from Heaven, there is much work to be done to prepare for that Day. It is not enough to believe a prophetic message. We must live a prophetic lifestyle.

Chapter 10

The Urgency of Love

"The end of all things is near; therefore, be serious and discipline yourselves for the sake of your prayers. Above all, maintain constant love for one another, for love covers a multitude of sins."
(1 Peter 4:7,8)

"Let your gentleness be evident to all. The Lord is near."
(Philippians 4:5)

No Little People, No Little Places

Elijah was God's champion in the big showdown on Mount Carmel with the 450 prophets of God's chump competition, Baal. I think it is significant to note what was happening for the three and a half years *prior* to the Big Rumble. While hiding from King Ahab, Elijah's life was mundane. He camped out in the desert near a stream and hung out in the home of a poor Gentile widow. His life would have been one boring reality show. But God performs miracles constantly, if we have eyes to see them.

During the drought that he had prophesied to Israel, Elijah was miraculously fed by ravens. He also became the miraculous means of provision for a starving widow and even raised her son from the dead. Even though they suffered from the very same judgments of God that Elijah had decreed for that region, God faithfully cared for them! Even as Yahweh is dealing with the deceived King Ahab and the compromise of the whole nation of Israel, He does not overlook the needs of one Gentile widow or His vagabond prophet! It may not get headlines in the world, but God is taking care of all who look to him in stunning ways every day. He will do it during the Great Tribulation at the end of the Age.

How we demonstrate dependence on God in the spectacular moments of our lives is a direct result of how we depend on God during our daily routines. Cultivating the kind of lifestyle that will endure great trials is cobbled during the myriad moments of leaning on God for little things.

There is an Elijah-like parallel in Jesus' life before His big show-down with all the powers of Heaven and Earth on Mount Moriah, the Jewish Temple Mount.

Toward the end of His three and a half year public ministry, Jesus was going through Jericho on the way to His death in Jerusalem. It would have been so easy for Him to be preoccupied with His fast approaching confrontation with cosmic powers; but He was not too busy or anxious to stop and heal a blind man named Bartimaeus, or to have lunch with a despised tax collector named Zacchaeus with a hungry heart for the Kingdom. Jesus was not so distracted with the big picture that He became blind to real human beings in his path. He cared about people. This is the Good Shepherd who leaves the 99 sheep already in a safe place to search for the one who is lost.

Jesus knew meeting immediate needs opens the human heart to the bigger need for eternity. In fact, the human heart is where God has *set* eternity. The value of one person and one act of kindness is never discounted in the economy of God.

Prophecy and the Lifestyle of Love

There is a natural tension between anticipating a future event and staying attentive to the present. This can play out on a grand scale in terms of how we live out the values of the King while antici-pating the arrival of His Kingdom. We don't want to fall in love with the God of the future and fail to obey the God of the next two min-utes. We need biblical bifocals. We need to develop a way of seeing life and history that keeps both near and far realities in focus. We don't want to fall into the ditch of emphasizing Bible prophecy and End-Times scenarios and forget to "do justly, love mercy, and walk humbly with our God" (Micah 6:8). We don't want to fall into the other ditch of meeting temporary felt human needs and forgetting that each person has an eternal destiny for which to prepare.

Many who care a lot about social justice in this Age think very little about the arrival of the Age to come. We must have a grip on both realities to be robustly Christ-like. If you care about eternity, you must care about whether people really know Jesus or not. The message preached by Peter in Acts chapter 4 is as true today as it was then. He proclaimed, "Salvation is found in no one else, for there is *no other name* under heaven, given among men, by which we *must* be saved" (Acts 4:12). Loving others demands that we warn them of coming judgment that they will be saved from it.

Peter and the first generation of messengers preached a very inclusive cure for what ails us all. The invitation to receive the forgiveness of God for sin was for everyone. But it only came through one person—Jesus of Nazareth. Since people don't like to humble themselves to anyone, that name got them in a lot of trouble then and will still get you in trouble today. Some people *hate* the name of Jesus. I assure you every demon in the Dark Kingdom does. Today people perceive the Gospel as *ex*clusive because salvation is only in proper relationship with Jesus personally. I have great news! If you are a sinner who wants forgiveness you can have it in the life- giving blood of Jesus! I can't help you if you want forgiveness in some other name. No one else has the power to cancel the spiritual death sentence for your sins.

The message we call the Gospel is really an invitation to be a part of the best of all futures. The Gospel of the Kingdom is about a real flesh and blood King and a real time and place Kingdom. If the Gospel of Jesus is merely disembodied truth principles then there is nothing to separate Christianity from any other philosophical system.

The first disciples weren't killed because they were preaching a different philosophy. They were killed for preaching a different *King*! Their message was *treason* to Caesar and *blasphemy* to Rabbinical Judaism. Their very lives and willingness to suffer and die reflected that they had died already to this world and its rulers. Jesus said we were to be His "witnesses." The Greek word for witness is the same one for martyr. He sends us to the very power brokers of the world system with a message that when properly communicated and clearly understood can definitely get you killed. Jesus is a massive threat to the caretakers of this Age and so is anyone who claims to follow Him. Our very lives are meant to be a *warning* of coming judgment. We were *meant* to suffer conflict.

We preach the Gospel of forgiveness in Jesus' Name, but that is not the controversial part of the message He gave us to proclaim. Psychologists preach the merits of forgiveness. The message of the Kingdom of God is about Jesus coming to TAKE OVER. That offends. The House of the Lord is in absolute conflict with every other house. Even though we labor for peace and justice as followers of the Bridegroom King, our goal is not "peaceful co-existence" based on compromising the knowledge of the One Living God. We labor to proclaim unconditional surrender to the Prince of Peace who alone will bring peace on Earth when He comes. Until then, conflict is our portion. To proclaim Jesus in the last generation will be treason to the Anti-Christ spirit of the Age.

Midnight in Egypt – Time to Surrender

Pharaoh of Egypt couldn't claim he had not been fully warned of the consequences of resisting God after ten heaven-sent plagues and a very persistent messenger in Moses. The people of the Earth in the last generation will have many warnings and shakings in order to surrender to the Great King before He comes. "God is not pleased that any should perish but that all should come to the knowledge of repentance" (2 Peter 3:9). Even though the Gospel is the best news ever, it is perceived as horrible news to those who don't want to hear it.

One can hardly watch TV, listen to news, or read any media and escape the cultural fascination with the end of the world. The movie "2012" combines virtually every cataclysmic event one can imagine! But while there is much warning language and imagery in modern media, the veracity of the ancient biblical version is typically trivialized or blended with other world religions and current philosophies.

Make no mistake, the Lord of History is warning the people of the Earth on every level. Nevertheless, as the Day of the Lord zooms closer, it will be you and me who bear the responsibility to articulate a clear message of warning to our neighbors and provide safe, praying communities for them.

The Gospel of a coming Kingdom, though 2000 years old, still is compelling and urgent. Take the terms of surrender to Jesus now and you will live as His citizen forever! Now is the time to surrender, because once He gets here it is too late.

Or suppose a king is about to go to war against another king. Will he not first sit down and consider whether he is able with ten thousand men to oppose the one coming against him with twenty thousand? If he is not able, he will send a delegation while the other is still a long way off and will ask for terms of peace. In the same way, any of you who does not give up everything he has cannot be my disciple. (Luke 14:31-33)

The gospel terms are amazing. You won't get a better deal! Turn from your life of sin, trust in the leadership of Jesus over your life, and be baptized into His community. Refuse and you will suffer the same fate as Pharaoh and his army who went to the bottom of the Red Sea. The Kingdom of Darkness is for people who, in their blind pride, *want* to go there in spite of all the signs and warnings they have been given along the way. No one will stand before God with a good excuse on the Day of Judgment.

Growing in Passion as the Bridegroom King Draws Near

Some four hundred plus years before Jesus came, Daniel read the words of Jeremiah the prophet and understood that the time of Israel's prophesied captivity in Babylon was about to end. Daniel did not sit back with a sense of passive inevitability. He was overcome with a passion to press in to fasting and prayer. The content of

Daniel's conversation with God was a cry for renewal of the Covenant that Yahweh had made with His people at Mount Sinai.

In the first year of (Darius) reign, I, Daniel, understood from the Scriptures, according to the word of the LORD given to Jeremiah, the prophet, that the desolation of Jerusalem would last seventy years. So I turned to the Lord God and pleaded with him in prayer and petition, in fasting, and in sackcloth and ashes. I prayed to the LORD my God and confessed:

O Lord, the great and awesome God, who keeps his covenant of love with all who love him and obey his commands, we have sinned and done wrong. We have been wicked and have rebelled; we have turned away from your commands and laws. We have not listened to your servants the prophets, who spoke in your name to our kings, our princes and our fathers, and to all the people of the land. (Daniel 9:1-6)

Daniel "*pleaded* in prayer." He identified with the corporate, cultural, multi-generational sins of his people. He prayed his way out of the delusion and apathy of his generation. He pressed in to the promises of God with *urgency* because he did not want God's Bridal People Israel to miss the moment of their destiny.

I believe all of God's Bridal People today are entering a season like the one in which Daniel lived. We, like Daniel, ought to be a people of prayer who understand the season in which we live and have the appropriate response to God's great covenant of love. If we see the time of our marriage to God drawing near, we will press in to His promises with greater perseverance.

Daniel read this prophecy of Jeremiah:

This is what the Lord says, "When seventy years are completed for Babylon, I will come to you and fulfill my gracious promise to bring you back to this place. For I know the plans I have for you" declares the Lord, "plans to prosper you and not to harm you, plans to give you a hope and a future. Then you will call upon Me and come and pray to Me and I will listen to you. You will seek Me and find Me when you seek Me with all of your heart." (Jeremiah 29:10-12)

God's plan for the Babylonian captivity was to produce deep longings and obedience once again in the heart of His Bride Israel. Daniel begins to contend in his own prayer-life for this very thing. We, like Daniel, cry out for our generation to know the hour of God's promised restoration in order to fall in love with Him and desire to obey Him fully all over again.

Jeremiah Bought a Field

Jeremiah lived in a generation prior to Daniel's. Jeremiah had the burden of the Lord to proclaim horrific coming judgment to a generation that was saying, "Peace, peace" and "All is well." God sustains the hearts of His prophets with a gripping vision of a glorious future on the other side of great judgment. The irony is that only the most genuinely hopeful human vessel can bear the burden of proclaiming terrible judgment. We proclaim a message that disturbs the comforted and comforts the disturbed. The judgment of God on Judah came in the form of a Babylonian invasion, the political superpower of the day. But even though Jeremiah knew that devastation was coming to Judah, God told him to buy a field. God tells His forerunner messengers to invest in the Earth now even as we proclaim great devastation ahead, because He has plans for "a hope and a future."

Jeremiah 32: 24-25:

See how the siege ramps are built up to take the city. Because of the sword, famine and plague, the city will be handed over to the Babylonians who are attacking it. What you said has happened, as you now see. And though the city will be handed over to the Babylonians, you, O Sovereign LORD, say to me, 'Buy the field with silver and have the transaction witnessed.'

The land, the people, and the covenant promises God has made are precious to Him. Even if there are few who are righteous in the land, as was Jeremiah in his generation in Israel, God calls His righteous ones to invest. God is a Real Estate Agent. He wants us to buy land! Even in the face of great judgments, God's people are to persevere in hope and invest when others are selling out.

Jesus invested in us at the cross. I would have to say it was the worst investment God ever made. But He didn't mind getting ripped off! Through red-blurred vision, Jesus looked at people like you and me and paid the price for a future that no one else discerned that day. I believe that future didn't even *exist* until He breathed his last breath.

Our lives in this Age won't always make sense. God may call His own to acts of courage and self-sacrifice that only make sense if there is a future that is seen beyond the insanity of the circumstances around us. Will followers of Jesus today have the vision to see the Kingdom coming when life is not abundant in terms of increasing prosperity? Do we have a faith that will hold us in a time of crisis and devastation? Do we know the God who shakes the earth in order to produce love and faith in the human heart? Yes, yes, and yes, if our faith is in the God of the Bible.

No other God tenderly forgave us through His precious Son on a bloody tree. Those who know they are loved this deeply, can now love others, in the gentleness and urgency of His love.

Chapter 11

The Continuity of
the Kingdom of God

"Let nothing move you.
Always give yourselves fully to the work of the Lord,
because you know that your labor in the Lord is not in vain."
(1 Cor. 15:58)

The Principal of Continuity

Regardless of one's view of how history will climax, I believe there is a principal of continuity in God's economy. In other words, the supernatural God of creation and history still honors cause and effect in the world He has made. What we do in real time matters. Actions have consequences. History is not a sham. Therefore a real Galilean man dying between the 3rd and 9th hours during a national religious holy feast on a real Roman cross outside the gates of a real Jewish capital city means something. The historical fact that on Sunday morning this same Man who was three days dead walked out of a rock tomb with a resurrected body means everything.

Matter matters. The material universe is sacred to God, too. He added molecules to His deity when He wrapped Himself in flesh in Mary's virgin womb. That is why every Christian ought to cry out for the unborn to be born. That is not just a lump of tissue in a woman's belly. That array of chemicals is ALIVE. You were once that miraculous living lump, just like Jesus.

The corrupted world that we understand and experience in this present Age will be the same one redeemed physically as well as spiritually in the Age to come. God made Creation "good." He loves the Earth we live in now and everything in it. He wants it back! His zeal for making all things new surpasses all human imagination. But the future Earth probably won't be some Dr. Seuss planet with polka dot trees that we won't recognize. It will be a much enhanced version of what we know now. Heaven and Earth version 2.0 is coming! This ought to motivate us to live with maximum faith, hope, and love in the One who owns it now.

Continuity means that if Jesus comes back in the next 40 years, my city of Birmingham will still be here. I might be, too. I want Jesus to be delighted with His Bride in Birmingham. I believe people and things that please Jesus in our city will pass into the next period of history under His government. Wicked things and wicked leaders will be destroyed, but much will be redeemed.

The Importance of the Global Prayer Movement

Because of the lateness of the hour and power of the delusion of our culture, I believe in the importance of giving ourselves more wholeheartedly to corporate prayer and worship. There are many cultural expressions of praying communities, but there has only been one prayer movement since the first conversation between God and Adam in the Garden. Every one of God's Bridal People through every Age has been a part of one growing conversation between God and His children.

God established a national prayer room for Israel in the tabernacle in the Sinai desert under Moses and later in Jerusalem under King David and his son King Solomon. But Jesus told a Samaritan woman at a well that true worship of God would no longer be limited to one place or one people. Jesus pronounced judgment on the corrupt Temple of His day because it was no longer serving the purpose for its creation. "My Father's house is to be a house of prayer for all Nations, but you have made it a den of thieves" (Matt

21:13). Jesus prophesied, "Destroy this temple, and I will raise it again in three days" (John 2:19). Through His resurrection, Jesus would create a new temple with the living stones of a new humanity called the Church.

Jesus is the Meeting Place.

Jesus wants us to be with Him where He is and He wants to be with us where we are. His current residence is in God's Throne Room above the Heavens. At Jesus' return the veil between our hearts and the Throne of God above the Heavens and Earth will be torn apart. Full fellowship will be visibly restored. The Spirit of God mediates the divine dialog between us until that Day.

If prayer is our real time conversation with Jesus on His Throne, that one concept will radicalize your whole understanding of prayer. Prayer is not the last thing you do because it is the most foolish and unproductive activity on your list. Prayer is your lifeline to God now and even in the Millennial Kingdom. Some form of prayer, which is simply our communication with Jesus the King, inevitably continues as we partner with Jesus in His ever increasing government around the world.

Get used to the conversation now! Get in rooms where Jesus is talking to a lot of us at the same time. It will blow your mind! Every time we gather in corporate prayer in what we call the Birmingham Prayer Furnace, I become a believer in prayer all over again. The room is often thick with life and crackling with the most vibrant communication I have ever experienced on this side of the Kingdom come. That "place of prayer" is what I miss when I am not there. It is so much better than any other communication format. I can't explain it and I can't control it. But there it is! That is why I know it isn't me, but the Spirit of God that is leading the meeting.

I also know that others in the room are connected by the Holy Spirit living in their deepest heart to God living on the Throne of Heaven. That kind of understanding will keep you pumped up when it is two people and nothing else but empty chairs! This thing we call prayer is when we participate for a few of our fleshly breaths with an eternal reality for which we were all born and destined. Why *wouldn't* there be a dynamic global prayer movement before Jesus comes back? He isn't returning for a bunch of folks that barely know Him or rarely talk to Him; He is coming for a pure and passionate Bride!

Today's global corporate prayer movement is also the same one that began forty days after Jesus' resurrection in Jerusalem. One hundred and twenty men and women praying in an upper room night and day for ten days after Jesus went back to Heaven were given power by the Holy Spirit to go public with the news of His forgiveness and His coming Kingdom.

That same power from God that went from the upper room prayer meeting to the streets of Jerusalem is what is available to every gathering of praying people today. Now God's Spirit is poured out on men and women, young and old! Every follower of Jesus becomes a citizen-priest with full access to God's Throne Room.

The prayer movement transcends and undergirds our church structures and communities. God wants to have intimate conversation with each and all of His children. As important and helpful as ministry structures may be, they are only the scaffolding of a much greater work of God throughout history. If we are honest, we will admit that the very structures we promote are sometimes more of an obstacle than a door connecting us to God's presence. All denominations, local churches, and organizations will pass away or be radically transformed when Jesus comes. We need to remember that so that we do not grow too fond of them.

One thing we know, God wants places of prayer where everyone with a hungry heart can encounter Him. We may not always have the luxury of buildings, bank accounts, and programs, but every one of us ought to know how to relate to Jesus out of our own heart. Anything that is not about growing intimacy with Him and participation in His Kingdom is not going to last.

Ears to Hear

If our hearts are alive, we instinctively know there is always more to reality than our experience of it. Jesus likes to give things to those who spend time with Him in that place of inquiry that comes from intimacy. What we need from Him most as His Bridal People are "ears to hear." We live in an information age, but we lack "understanding." People who pray and ask Jesus lots of questions are the ones who get lots of answers. If we understand the Reformation Age, or Renaissance, and the 20th Century, but do not understand what Jesus says about this time called NOW, we have become dull and don't even know it.

Right now counts. What you do after you read this chapter counts. That is why we need to be in constant dialog with the Holy Spirit, who is our link to the heart and mind of Jesus. That is why prayer is important. Because of the "Principle of Continuity," the life we live now counts. The justice we fight for now counts. The lives and marriages and institutions that reflect God's beautiful character now will set the tone for the next generation, if not the beginning of the Millennial Kingdom itself. Will Jesus have a lot to work with when He comes? I believe He will! I am motivated to give Him more. The people who love Jesus now will be the ones He gives authority to in the Kingdom coming with Him.

Praise awaits you O God in Zion; to you our vows will be fulfilled. O you who hear prayer, to you all men will come. Blessed are those you choose and bring near to live in your courts! (Psalm 65:1,2,4)

Loving Justice while Preaching the Kingdom

If we long for the Bridal City and her King and believe that how we live today will affect the quality of the future and our eternity, we will stay engaged in persevering love for God's world and all its inhabitants. Some people believe that only human souls will remain in eternity. God takes physical creation and human communities seriously in His plans for redemption, too. Jesus says, in the judgment of the nations after His return in Matthew Chapter 25, that how we treat one another, especially the least and most despised among us will determine whether we belong in His Kingdom or not.

When the Son of Man comes in his glory, and all the angels with him, he will sit on his throne in heavenly glory. All the nations will be gathered before him, and he will separate the people one from another as a shepherd separates the sheep from the goats. He will put the sheep on his right and the goats on his left.

Then the King will say to those on his right, 'Come, you who are blessed by my Father; take your inheritance, the kingdom prepared for you since the creation of the world. For I was hungry and you gave me something to eat, I was thirsty and you gave me something to drink, I was a stranger and you invited me in, I needed clothes and you clothed me, I was sick and you looked after me, I was in prison and you came to visit me.'

Then the righteous will answer him, "Lord, when did we see you hungry and feed you, or thirsty and give you something to drink? When did we see you a stranger and invite you in, or needing clothes and clothe you? When did we see you sick or in prison and go to visit you?"

The King will reply, "I tell you the truth, whatever you did for one of the least of these brothers of mine, you did for me."

Then he will say to those on his left, "Depart from me, you who are cursed, into the eternal fire prepared for the devil and his angels. For I was hungry and you gave me nothing to eat, I was thirsty and you gave me nothing to drink, I was a stranger and you did not invite me in, I needed clothes and you did not clothe me, I was sick and in prison and you did not look after me."

They also will answer, "Lord, when did we see you hungry or thirsty or a stranger or needing clothes or sick or in prison, and did not help you?"

He will reply, "I tell you the truth, whatever you did not do for one of the least of these, you did not do for me."

Then they will go away to eternal punishment, but the righteous to eternal life. Matt 25:31-46

Some today would say that this passage refers to how Gentile nations are judged in terms of their treatment of the biological brothers of Jesus, the Jewish people. The problem with that view is that by particularizing "the least of these my brothers" to mean *only* ethnic Israel, we can unwittingly justify mistreating others for the sake of the secular Jewish nation today. While anti-Semitism is wrong, it is wrong in precisely the same way that hatred toward *any* marginalized group of human beings is wrong. The view most in line with the Sermon on the Mount value system of Mathew five, six, and seven is to apply Matthew 25 as Mother Teresa did when she "saw the face of Jesus" in the destitute and dying on the streets of Calcutta. *All* human beings are beloved image-bearers of God.

God says how we treat the poor and marginalized of any society is a sign of the way we treat *Him*. Every act of faith toward Jesus will be remembered and rewarded in the Age to come. We should not try to dodge that bullet as much as we would like to. The evaluation we receive when we stand before Jesus will include our personal *and* corporate involvement in the value system of His Kingdom of justice and righteousness. Nations will be judged as well as individuals. "Soul-winning" is wise. So is instructing souls won to live by the King's values.

Chapter 12

Foundations of Creation and Government

*"For to us a Child is born, to us a Son is given, and the govern-
ment will be on His shoulders. And He will be called Wonderful
Counselor, Mighty God, Everlasting Father, Prince of Peace. Of
the increase of His government and peace there will be no end. He
will reign on David's Throne and over his kingdom, establishing
justice and righteousness from that time on and forever. The zeal of
the Lord Almighty will accomplish this."*
(Isaiah 9:6-7)

Justice, Righteousness, and Shalom

When we are talking about the Millennial Kingdom of Jesus,
we must lay a foundation for how the Bible defines justice
and righteousness. These two words are often used together. They
are indivisible realities that make up the very core of God's nature
and thus the basis of His Government and Creation itself.

*The Lord reigns, let the Earth be glad: let the distant shores rejoice.
Clouds and thick darkness surround Him; righteousness and justice
are the foundation of His throne.* (Psalm 97:1-2)

Together, righteousness and justice constitute "shalom."

This Hebrew word "shalom," which we translate "peace" is more dynamic than our common understanding of the English word. Shalom represents a harmony between God, His creation, and all living things. It is more than the absence of conflict, it is the fullness of God's Presence defining all things in their right relationship to one another. It is what the Messianic Kingdom on earth and New Creation will be like.

I will make a covenant of peace with them and rid the land of wild beasts so that they may live in the desert and sleep in the forests in safety. I will bless them and the places surrounding my hill. I will send down showers in season; there will be showers of blessing. The trees of the field will yield their fruit and the ground will yield its crops; the people will be secure in their land. . . They will know that I, the Lord their God, am with them and that they, the House of Israel, are My People, declares the Sovereign Lord. (Ezekiel 34:25-27, 30)

Now the dwelling of God is with men, and He will live with them. They will be His people and God Himself will be with them and be their God. He will wipe every tear from their eyes. There will be no more death or mourning or crying or pain, for the old order of things has passed away." (Rev. 21:3-4)

Let not the wise man boast of his strength or the rich man boast of his riches, but let him who boasts boast about this: that he under-stands and knows Me, that I am the LORD, who exercises kindness, justice and righteousness on Earth, for in these I delight declares the LORD. (Jeremiah 9:23-24)

Though justice and righteousness share deep overlapping concepts of moral perfection between God, Men, and each other, they are not mere similes. Justice is primarily right relationships between Adam's children. Justice is the moral leveler and straight edge. Righteousness is about right relationships between human beings but with more of a conscious connection with our Heavenly Dad. Righteousness is the moral plumb line. "I will make justice the measuring line and righteousness the plumb line'" (Isaiah 28:17). Both justice and righteousness include vertical and horizontal dimensions which reveal true Human and Divine natures but in different ways.

The best civil laws are both just and righteous. Biblical social justice and biblical personal righteousness is what Christians must model, preach, and contend for in the moral chaos of our culture. The current Civil and Human Rights movement has been hijacked by those who wed secular concepts of social justice to concepts of personal unrighteousness. If secular forces successfully redefine morality in civil law in terms of convenient human opinion, their victory will only speed social disintegration. The God of Creation and Law is morally pure and righteous. No society can abandon the justice and righteousness of Jesus' Kingdom and endure with greatness.

Religion and Politics

All governments are held accountable to God to execute justice regardless of their belief systems—religious or otherwise. The Bible reveals God as the One who raises kingdoms up and who tears kingdoms down. All kingdoms. One of the primary purposes of any civic government is to enforce social order through guarding and promoting peace with justice. You do not have to be a Christian to recognize this. Parents who practice witchcraft discipline their kids when they are "bad." Jesus said "Render to Caesar," not "Burn down Rome."

In Romans 13:1-7, civil governments have the full stamp of God to maintain justice and punish evil-doers, but these same governments do not have the responsibility to promote His Name or His worship. The best they can do is not hinder religious freedom. It is the responsibility of the followers of Jesus to represent the God of the Bible. This role cannot be delegated to civil authorities.

If you are Muslim, there is no final line of separation between "religion and state." The goal of Islam in this era, and thus its vision of the Millennium, is to establish codes of conduct through the State based on the Quran. This type of law, or "sharia," includes penalties for "wrong" worship. Look no further than any predominantly

Muslim society and tell me if I am mistaken. Islam is committed to the creation of Muslim nation states until the whole world is "Dar-ul-Islam," which in Arabic means, the House of Islam. Conquest is what Muhammad taught and modeled.

Even moderate Muslims are committed to global government under Quranic values and codes. The radical and moderate Muslim may differ in methodology, but the goal is the same. Can there be any great mystery about why democracy, or rule by the people, is in fundamental tension with Islamic ideals of theocracy or rule by God?

The Judeo-Christian tradition also has theocracy as its great vision of the future. But in these traditions, only the coming Messiah can create such a government promised to Israel's King David. There will finally be peace in Jerusalem and around the world.

Long after David's reign, the Hebrew prophet Ezekiel wrote about the future, "I will place over them one shepherd. I the Lord will be their God and my servant David will be prince among them. I the Lord have spoken" (Ezekiel 34:23-24).

It is my belief that there is no such thing as a truly biblical Christian nation-state today. The Christian nation is the global Church. Followers of Jesus are the "kingdom of priests and holy nation" Peter talked about in 1 Peter 2:9. That is also how Yahweh described His vision of Israel to Moses on Mount Sinai in Ex. 19:6. "One nation under God" is a nice phrase in the American pledge of allegiance, but that phrase fully belongs only to God's Covenant People around the globe through every generation.

The U.S. Declaration of Independence proclaims inalienable rights of life, liberty, and the pursuit of happiness. The Bible proclaims that God alone has rights, but He extends great mercy and love to all in order that all might pursue holiness in this Age to possess unspeakable happiness in the next.

There are various nations who have, or have had, strong Judeo-Christian influences, but Jesus did not mandate that his followers should create Christian political states in the Church Age. He declared to Rome at His trial before Pilate, "My Kingdom is not of this world, if it were my disciples would fight for me" (John 18:36).

136

The current mandate of the Kingdom of God until Jesus returns is found in the Sermon on the Mount. "You are the salt of the Earth. . . You are the light of the World. . . Let your light shine before men, that they may see your good deeds and praise your Father in Heaven" (Matthew 5:13-14).

Should followers of Jesus be involved in civil politics? Answer these questions. Do you care about justice and righteousness for all, not just yourself? Do you want to see public policies that are based on biblical truths and principles? Do you want to preserve a culture that guarantees basic human rights including the freedom to "change religions"? If the answer is yes, then followers of Jesus should attempt to be salt (slowing down injustice and unrighteousness) and light (promoting justice and righteousness) in every sphere of society, including civil government.

When Jesus promised He would return to set up a government that would never end, it wasn't so we would disengage from changing the world we live in now. We don't lie dormant as a secret society never practicing the cultural values of God's Kingdom in the open and suddenly get high ranking offices in the Age to come. True Christianity will always have a positive transformational influence in any culture through redeemed hearts willing to suffer for truth and love for Jesus' sake.

Christians look to the thirty-nine Jewish books of the Old Testament as equally inspired with the twenty-seven books of the New Testament. Therefore the powerful examples of God's covenant people serving in pagan or secular governments still speak. Joseph rose from prison to serve at the right hand of Pharaoh in Egypt. Daniel excelled above his Babylonian classmates to serve in high offices of three regimes in Medo-Persia. These are relevant paradigms for followers of Jesus today.

God clearly wants justice and righteousness in every government. It is what causes nations to prosper and endure. If God's people are the salt of the Earth and light of the World then our influence needs to be everywhere. Having said this, I hasten to say, that the primary role of the follower of Jesus is not to help run institutions, as important as that might be. The primary role of those who know and love Jesus is to live and die as prophetic signposts of a greater Kingdom coming. Why? Because the World as we know it is dying until He comes.

Millennial Visions and Social Transformation

Martin Luther King, Jr. never held a political office, yet his voice and willingness to suffer with others for the cause of racial and economic justice changed the world in the 1950s and '60s. He did it as a young Bible believing Baptist preacher. Did he learn some of his principles of non-violent revolution from Gandhi, a Hindu? Yes. But Gandhi learned them from the Bible and from Jesus. Dr. Martin Luther King, Jr. like Gandhi, courageously applied Jesus' Sermon on the Mount principles such as "do not resist an evil person" and "turn the other cheek" to the politics of his generation.

Did Martin Kingandotherleadersin theCivil Rightsmovement practice personal unrighteousness in the form of sexual infidelity? Regrettably, yes. Few of King's defenders would continue to deny the sad facts. But those moralists who point out that King did not live a spotless life should not use King's personal failures as an excuse to ignore how God used him to inspire a globe for the sake of civil justice and racial healing. It was the dream of the Millennium of Jesus' rule and Hebraic biblical shalom, that caused King and others to coin the term "The Beloved Community" and contend forAmerica to live up to that higher vision of the Kingdom of God.

I believe the Beloved Community ideal is needed once again in our day, only more fully expressed in a biblical and Christ-centered way than even King and his generation were able to do. Obeying Jesus Christ includes working for justice but not only "social justice." The Beloved Community of Jesus'Kingdom cherishes God's standards of social justice AND God's standards of personal righteousness. The current secular human rights movement includes many human wrongs. When human rights are about honoring others made in God's image, according to God's design, that is right. When human "rights" include destroying other humans in the womb, waging unjust wars, character assassination in the media, pornography as protected free speech, exploiting the poor in the name of corporate profits, participating in global sex traffic, or tearing down the foundations of the nuclear family to promote same sex marriage, those are not rights at all. That is evil masquerading as good.

We can have a big house in a peaceful neighborhood with full social privileges and still not finish life well. We do not have a "right" to go to Heaven. That is a gift. God has the right to our full obedience. When Jesus comes He will assert God's right to be worshipped by all flesh. Hell is not run by the Devil. Hell was made by God to institute the will of men and angels who do not honor the just, right, and true leadership of Jesus.

Jesus said, "Do not be afraid of those who kill the body but cannot kill the soul. Rather, be afraid of the One who can destroy both soul and body in hell" (Matthew 10:28).

In our global culture of designer religion we mix and match our values and truths to suit our own tastes. Many would say that someone who lives the values of Jesus but who does not acknowledge Him as the Lord of All will still finish life well. Jesus did tell stories like the Good Samaritan to illustrate how God values being a good neighbor. But we are never saved by doing good simply because none of us is ever good *enough*. We are saved by a Person, not a stat sheet. Can we live the values of Jesus, deny His name, and still finish well when we stand before Him? No.

Salvation is found in no one else, for there is no other name under heaven given among men by which we must be saved. (Acts 4:12)

For whoever is ashamed of Me and my words in this adulterous and sinful generation, of him will the Son of Man also be ashamed when He comes in the glory of His Father with the holy angels. (Mark 8:38)

There are millions of people who name the Name of Jesus, who have prayed a prayer, responded to an altar call, been "filled with the Holy Ghost" and spoken in tongues, or been declared a Christian by rite of church membership or baptism who do not evidence the values of Jesus by how they treat others. Can we name the Name of Jesus, deny His values, and still finish well when we stand before Him? No.

Not everyone who says to me, 'Lord, Lord,' will enter the kingdom of heaven, but only he who does the will of my Father who is in heaven. Many will say to me on that day, 'Lord, Lord, did we not prophesy in your name, and in your name drive out demons and perform many miracles?' Then I will tell them plainly, 'I never knew you. Away from me, you evildoers!' (Matthew 7:21-23)

Loving Jesus and living His values are both required to finish life and history well. He is the full embodiment of justice, righteousness, and truth. As the Prince of Peace, He alone brings the fullness of shalom to our fragmented world.

Chapter 13

One Kingdom,
One Value System, One Future

"But our citizenship is in heaven. And we eagerly await a
Savior from there, the Lord Jesus Christ."
(Phil. 3:20)

Two Prophetic Voices of America's Last Century

D r. King is memorialized as a "Drum Major" for the gospel of social justice. One of his contemporaries, evangelist Billy Graham, was primarily known as America's prophetic voice for the gospel of personal salvation.

King's message was a prophetic voice calling for a "realized eschatology" out of an Amillennial view of history. He was preaching for more of the justice and righteousness of Heaven to be realized in his generation on a national social level. Graham's message played better among those who hardly felt a need for social justice at all. They were more concerned about going to Heaven after they died. Their awareness of personal guilt and the need to be forgiven for the condition of their soul before a Holy God filled stadiums for decades. Many of these same people were puzzled by why all the "Negroes" were so upset.

In the South during this era, you had tent meeting revivals on one side of town drawing huge crowds of one ethnicity for evangelical personal encounters with God and on the other side of town you had mass meetings of ecstatic worship, prayer, and preaching that galvanized people of another ethnicity into social action for cultural transformation. Both messages were authentically biblical even though the people attending the meetings barely knew each other or often hated and feared each other.

How do we Define "Revival"?

I live in a Southern City where false dichotomies pitting concepts of justice and righteousness against each other are still played out in our church communities. I have had conversations with elder church leaders in both black and white communities recounting the "revivals" of our city over the last several decades and no mention is given at all to the year of 1963.

What happened in Birmingham in 1963? The whole tide of the faltering Civil Rights movement turned when one of the greatest men this city ever knew, the Rev. Fred Shuttlesworth, invited Dr. King and his movement to confront Police and Fire Commissioner Bull Connor and the powers of brutal racism that existed here. Even that campaign nearly died while King sat behind bars and wrote what later became known as the "Letter from a Birmingham Jail" to rebuke the sleeping Church of my city.

It was only when a risky call went out for the Black children of Birmingham to leave school to march in the demonstrations downtown that the back of racial segregation was broken. National television news cameras captured images of children and teenagers being blasted with fire hoses and set upon with German Shepherd police dogs. These "Black and White" TV broadcasts caused the conscience of America to shift on the race issue in a matter of minutes.

After the breakthrough in Birmingham in the spring, Martin King would preach the "I Have a Dream Speech" from the Lincoln Memorial in Washington, DC that August. On September 15, back in Birmingham, the Klan bombed the 16th Street Baptist Church, killing four girls and putting a cork on the new well of justice opened months before.

The next year Billy Graham came to Birmingham to hold his first integrated evangelistic crusade in the South in Legion Field. This was the stadium where the famous Auburn – Alabama Iron Bowl was played every year. Despite threats of violence, Graham refused to cancel the meeting. Billy Graham later recalled how the Ku Klux Klan knocked out the crusade signs. Police escorts accompanied Graham everywhere for fear he would be shot. But the integrated crowd of 30,000 was peaceful. According to author John Pollack, "National press reporters were stunned at the response, when blacks and whites together streamed forward at the invitation."

Revival begins with personal repentance and empowerment from the Holy Spirit. Prophetic voices arise catalyzing movements that go on to transform cultures as well. Fifty years later, our generation is in desperate need of genuine spiritual awakening. Yet God is at work. There is reason to hope for biblical change in the spiritual crisis of our generation. I believe that as wells of justice, righteousness, and truth dug by earlier generations are re-dug, those uncorked wells release spiritual awakening into the next generation.

Like any city, Birmingham today faces deep cultural challenges that spring from the depravity of sinful human hearts. But those who are forgiven much, love much. For decades the Church of our city has quietly been transcending racial and cultural barriers that had us bound in hatred and prejudice. Our current police chief is an amazing African-American leader. For years, Chief A. C. Roper has led monthly police escorted worship and prayer walks through the highest crime neighborhoods. Violent crime rates have significantly declined.

When I think of Chief Roper of today and Chief Bull Connor of yesterday, righteousness has "roped the bull" of unrighteousness. Prayer Force United is policing the spiritual powers over our city through intercessory prayer to assist those who use physical and legal authority to restrain evil. What a different picture of Birmingham's police from the racist brutality of 1963!

On April 27, 2011, a terrible outbreak of tornadoes brought international attention to great loss of life and property in Alabama. But the rapid and sustained mobilization of the Christian community to respond to the human crisis was nothing less than stunning.

I sat in rooms with black and white leaders who, without a thought, deferred to one another for the sake of doing what was right, doing it in a right way, and doing it right away. I am proud to be a part of the Body of Christ in Birmingham, Alabama, a city once covered in shame before the eyes of the world. By re-digging wells of justice, we are contending for the Birmingham of Jesus' dreams.

Every generation of the People of God are called to live Jesus' Kingdom values based on justice, righteousness, and truth on a social level, *AND* justice, righteousness, and truth on a personal level. I believe a generation is on the scene right now that will do exactly that. But the irony is this: if this generation on the Earth today *IS* the last generation before Jesus' return, all their rightly motivated actions to serve others will be finally opposed by a global Anti-Christ government that will hate them not on the issue of humanitarian activity, but on the issue of worship. A global political system in this Age may bring a skewed form of justice and "peace," but it will not produce right worship and it will not be the true shalom of the Age to come.

A New Pharaoh Comes on the Scene

During Joseph's day in Egypt, the Hebrew nation had a pretty cushy life in the land of Cush as they called their neighborhood. But a Pharaoh came along who did not know Joseph or care about the contributions of the Hebrews. This Pharaoh saw God's Covenant People as a threat to his power monopoly fueled by the cult of Pharaoh worship, so he made life more and more unbearable for them through slavery.

It became necessary for God to send a deliverer in the person of Moses to try to persuade Pharaoh to allow the Israelites freedom to worship Yahweh. Right worship of the true God was becoming impossible in Egypt under this ruler. The new pharaoh was a fore-runner of the global Anti-Christ Ruler to come.

I believe a world monopoly on pseudo- "righteousness and justice" under the deception of a powerful mixture of humanitarianism and a compromised global religion will be the final ploy in Satan's grand scheme to wrest worship away from the Holy One of Israel to himself through his puppet king. World opinion will lump lovers of Jesus with "fundamentalists" of every other sect and religion. That process is underway as I write.

Anyone in America who does not buy wholeheartedly into the current ascendant homosexual and humanistic cultural agenda is a candidate for that list today. The drive to paint all who resist this agenda as racists and bigots will mask the real intolerance of the eschatology of those who believe Man is the captain of his own fate. That movement will escalate when international politics, economics, and increasing natural disasters force the world into a new global religion that supports the new world order.

The high stakes subtlety of this deception is going on right now. Do-goodism is seen as self-evident to the undiscerning mind. Anyone against "world peace," "humanitarian sentiment," and the mish-mashed "one world religion" will become an enemy of the global state. Anyone not worshipping this system and its leader will suffer for it. Cycles of social reformations are needed, but they will never be enough. The prophetic voice for personal and social change will ultimately give way to an apocalypse where the world will be born again under the leadership of Jesus.

Dividing Lines

The clash of kingdoms is demonstrated in ancient Babylon when three of Daniel's friends refused to bow in worship to the statue of Nebuchadnezzer in Daniel chapter three. When commanded to worship an idol of gold or die, Shadrach, Meshach, and Abednego replied:

"O Nebuchadnezzar, we do not need to defend ourselves before you in this matter. If we are thrown into the blazing furnace, the God we serve is able to rescue us from it, and He will rescue us from your hand, O king. But even if He does not, we want you to know, O king, that we will not serve your gods or worship the image of gold you have set up." (Dan 3:16-18)

I can imagine the rationale of the other Hebrews and captives from all over the world who were in Babylon. "Come on, just join the crowd! No harm to it. You can still bow to Yahweh in your heart. Look at all the good that has come from the Babylonian government. We have a form of world peace. Don't rock the boat."

Shadrach, Meshach, and Abednego chose rather to stand in a furnace than be forced to participate in the false worship of their day. The text shows they were perfect citizens of Babylon up to that point. But on that day they knew that a short life now for an eternal life to come was far better than to retire with a fat pension far from home. They were prepared to die on the worship issue. A fourth man like an angel stood with them in the fire. I believe it was the Son of God before his conception in Mary's womb.

Why do I believe the "one who looked like a son of man" walking with them in the furnace was Jesus? Because His unfolding historic identity and leadership has become the dividing line for *every* generation since He walked out of the Garden Tomb. The Person and Government of Jesus is the dividing line today. Dying for the One who sits on the highest Throne of Heaven is something that each person needs to settle in their own heart now, whether things appear rosy or bleak. A Bridal People not ready to die for Her Bridegroom King on the issue of first love is not ready to live for Him either.

I believe this is a picture of the developing scenario of the Bride of Jesus in the last hour of this Age. Even though followers of Jesus will always be giving themselves to serve God and Man, the time will come when global humanity's false worship will be required — or else. The problem with evil is that it can be disguised as goodness and doesn't show its true identity until the trap door is shut. The degree of subtlety and craftiness of the last human government before Jesus returns will be disarming to all but those most intimate with the true King.

For false Christs and false prophets will appear and perform great signs and miracles to deceive even the elect – if that were possible. (Matthew 24:24)

I believe a global night and day prayer movement is a necessary part of God's strategy to keep His people awake and fully engaged with His heart. In Revelation 12:10, the Accuser of God's Bridal People never stops lying to us. So if our Enemy never stops the dark dialog, whispering right in our ear, why do we think we can disengage from dialoging with the Holy Spirit 24-7?

Chapter 14
Art, Philosophy, Religion, Culture, and Visions of the Future

"As some of your own poets have said, 'We are his offspring.'"
(Acts 17:28)

The Battle of Millennial Messengers

Every religion, philosophy, and sci-fi story has one thing in common—a vision of the future. Who does the future belong to? What will it look like? How will we get there? Will human history end well or poorly? Where is God in the picture, if there is a god?

Christianity 101 teaches all things will come under the leadership of Jesus Christ, the rightful heir of the Universe. It is simply a matter of time.

And He made known to us the mystery of His will according to His good pleasure, which He purposed in Christ, to be put into effect when the times will have reached their fulfillment – to bring all things in heaven and on earth together under one head, even Christ. (Ephesians 1:9-10)

That one claim creates a massive conflict with every other competing universal system of thought! Not every religion is monotheistic. Eastern Religions have a different view of history and reality altogether. Instead of a linear view of history moving toward a climax under one God as Judaism, Islam, and Christianity teach, Buddhism, Hinduism, and New Age philosophies have a cyclical view of reality. In general terms, their hope is to escape the unending suffering of this world into a happy hunting ground of bliss, oneness with the universe, or even oblivion of the soul.

If you look at the three great monotheistic faiths, Jesus is the big dividing point. Rabbinical Judaism rejects Jesus of Nazareth as their Messiah, Islam says he is no more than a prophet, while Christianity says our eternal destiny depends on whether we have a personal relationship with Him.

Dang! Why does it have to be so confusing! Why are we put in such a difficult position where we have to search for the truth in a world where there are so many competitors for our worship? Many people decide on some subconscious level that all religions are basically the same and adopt one as a veneer or tradition. It is a path of least resistance. Most people around the Western world, regardless of religious affiliation, are secular humanists. They live with a lack of certainty about a Supreme Being while cobbling out the best material island of happiness they can construct. It is a form of God-denial. It is "Plan B." If there is no God of the 66 Books, this philosophy works well with the Spirit of the Age.

I do not recommend it. God has set eternity in the heart of every living person and we can never be truly happy apart from Him. You can try, but there is no running away from the ultimate questions of human existence. Even if you claim none of the recognized world religions, you still have a concept of "god" and of the future of human history. One of my friends was staking his future on UFOs and aliens being behind our existence. Hmmm. I wonder who is behind the existence of the aliens?

As we consider the Millennium of the Bible, I also want to look at the powerful cultural versions of the future being promoted through art and cinema. Jesus was a master communicator in His day. He was a walking Steven Spielberg movie. When He spoke, He spoke with authority, dramatic simplicity, and with special effects that caused audiences to marvel about whether He was the Messiah.

He got country folk to think big about their times and dream God- sized dreams about their role in the greatest storyline of all — human history.

Like it or not, movies and media are the parables of our generation. If you do not know who the character John Locke is from the TV series, *Lost*, you are, well. . . "lost' to one of the main cultural parables of the last decade. I believe we need to discern modern media through a biblical lens. Like the parables of Jesus, they are not necessarily obvious in their message. Those who came to Jesus with questions after the meeting were the ones who were given the parables meaning. I want to do that with some of the movies and literature of the past 150 years. As we dialog with Jesus about these modern day parables, I believe He will give us keys to understanding His heart for our times.

The Matrix Trilogy - Action Movie or Parable of our Times?

I realize that not everyone enjoys the same movies. Some of my friends never got into the *Matrix* trilogy of movies produced by the Wachowski brothers several years back. One walked out after the first scene, it was so dark and depressing to him.

Nonetheless, the *Matrix* series became a cultural icon for a significant period of time, which is a remarkable feat in this fast- paced, confusing world we live in. That was part of the genius behind the writing of the story. The movies were fast paced and confusing like us. But like the TV series *Lost*, there was enough skillful use of terms and images borrowed from every world religion and philosophy that it struck deep subconscious chords in us.

The mish-mash of imagery and sometimes corny (aren't we taking ourselves *way* too seriously now) dialog hinted that there was something about this movie that was intended to be a parable of our "Post-modern" generation.

Post-modern is the term used to describe an epoch shift in our collective philosophy and attitude as a westernized culture. After centuries of putting our trust in our own ability to think ourselves out of our messes with one stunning human improvement after another, we have become more pessimistic that science and technology and the next great management seminar will save us. We are turning instead to all kinds of "spirituality" to fashion a world that makes sense and has a happy ending.

For some, the *Matrix* series worked simply as an action and romance story. Lots of sensual passion, explosions, stylistic gun battles, cool sci-fi special effects, and martial arts. We love that stuff. Make the computer game. Move on. But whether they meant to or not, the Walchowski brothers stumbled on to several deeply biblical concepts, which is why it held the fascination of some of us in the Jesus community. But the Matrix is not a "Christian" movie as some may think.

The "Ubermensch" is Coming!

One of the "fathers" of what we now know as the Post-modern era, was a German philosopher named Friedrich Nietzsche. He was quite sure in his mind that the God of the Bible was not the real God of the universe and the sooner we shed the antiquated idea of him the better for all of us.

In the 3rd *Matrix* movie, "Trinity" the name of "Neo's" lover dies. It is hard for Neo (the New Man) to let go of Trinity (the Christian concept of God), but he must in order to fulfill his destiny and save "Zion" (the remaining free Human Race) from the mastery of Agent Smith (a fast multiplying "anti-Neo") and a race of intelligent machines who only like us for our electrical generating capacity. The poetic implication here is that the New Man must let a dead Trinity go to fulfill his true destiny.

This is a very "Post-modern" or Nietzschean concept of the Age we are living in today in the secular West. Let's discard the illusion of the God concepts that have served us in the past and embrace without fear or delusion that we as a race, in order to survive, must determine our own destiny in a universe without real moral boundaries.

One of Nietzsche's beliefs was that the highest concept of "god" was actually a society of people embodied by the idea of "Ubermench." In English, Superman. His philosophy was set out in his book "Thus Spake Zarathustra" in 1883.

In the old DC Comic version of Superman played out on black and white TV, you might recall the famous, "Look! Up in the sky! It's a bird! It's a plane! It's Superman! Able to leap tall buildings with a single bound, faster than a speeding bullet, more powerful than a locomotive," and so on.

Does this sound familiar to anyone who saw the first *Matrix* installment? Neo is first given training in the "jump program" which is essentially how to leap tall buildings with a single bound. Then Neo is told by his trainer, Morpheus (the name of the dude in mythology who was the gatekeeper to the dream world) that when he begins to really figure out his own superpowers, Neo won't have to dodge bullets. His speed relative to bullets will be far, far greater. Neo will be faster than a speeding bullet. Then there is a scene where Neo battles his nemesis, Agent Smith, in a subway station and basically ends up being more powerful than a locomotive.

If that isn't enough, in the last scene of the first movie, Neo steps out of a phone booth and begins to fly through the air! Can there be any doubt, that the Wachowski's are painting Neo as a type of Superman with Nietzsche's "Ubermensch" brush? While Nietzsche's Superman (or Over-man, more literally) is not one of superhuman *physical* strength, the Neo character can be viewed as a symbol of the Over-man's disregard for the necessity of God, and of his reliance upon his own humanity to conquer and survive.

You don't have to agree with me on that point. The real point isn't about a movie. The real point is about us and what we really believe about how human history will end. Will we finish well as a race? Does a New Millennial Golden Age stand ahead of us? If so, what will it be like?

If the cosmos is like astrophysicist and popular atheist speaker Stephen Hawking says, the material world is all there is. When we die our brains shut down like a computer. Eventually the universe will fade away with eternal expansion or, implode and start all over again. Either way we are probably fine for the next several billion years if we don't pollute the planet too much, cut down all the rain forests, blow ourselves up in a nuclear nightmare, melt the polar ice caps, or get taken out by an asteroid. We're safe enough, but our grandkids to the nth power are in some deep doo-doo.

Human Determinism

We all know we are in some deep doo-doo as a human race. If you don't know this, I can't help you! But if you are living in the same universe I am, we have major problems.

Whether you have ever heard of Friedrich Nietzsche or not means nothing. The fact is, our age of optimism and reason, "Modernity," has been seriously dented by a philosophic crisis of "faith" in the Western world. After two massive world wars, a stand-off between two nuclear superpower nations, and a growing threat of global terrorism with weapons of mass destruction, those of us who are awake enough to smell the coffee realize there is a reason why even secular prognosticators have the "Doomsday Clock" set at a few minutes to Midnight. Where is Neo when we need him?

When you basically rule out any serious consideration of the God of the Bible being able to actually *do* anything, then the world of "realpolitik" or some other "faith system" is the basket where you are putting your hopes for a happy ending.

The *Matrix* Trilogy is about human determinism, not Christian Theism. Neo finally "got it." The future rested squarely in his ability to believe something about himself and act on that belief. However, the interesting thing about how the trilogy ends is that it basically lays out the same conclusion as the 66 Books. I find it intriguing when other faith systems, in order to finish their story, can't help but tell the one that is already in the Bible.

Using the Bible

Louis Farrakhan is famous as the former leader of the Nation of Islam, or Black Muslim sect in America. In order to combat a horrible system of racism by European descended whites of "Christian" belief, he followed his leader, Elijah Muhammad, who established an equally racist reaction to corrupt Christianity for African-Americans using bits and pieces of classical Islam. When Farrakhan called for the Million Man March in the mid 1990s on the National Mall in Washington DC, he called it a "National Day of Atonement."

I have read the Qu'ran numerous times. I have had extensive inter-faith dialog with Muslim leaders and friends. Believe me, there is no clear concept of "atonement" in the Qu'ran, the authoritative book of Islam. There is no salvation by proxy where God accepts the death of one person as payment for the guilt of another. There is a feast, Idi Korbon, which recognizes putting guilt on a goat and sending it away, but it is a very far cry from the atoning sacrifice of Jesus on the cross for the sins of the world. Followers of Jesus and those who claim Muhammad was God's final prophet can agree on many concepts. But one that is absent from the Qu'ran and present throughout the Bible is the idea of "blood atonement."

Farrakhan is a very clever man to use a distinctively biblical idea, but give it non-biblical meaning for his own social agenda. Religious leaders, politicians, humanities professors, the Wachowski brothers, and many other Hollywood movie makers do the same. They know a good idea when they see it. Our Post-Christian culture is getting better at using concepts and language from the 66 Books to spin their own un-biblical stories. Undiscerning Christians get carried right along.

What Neo Discovered

Neo found faith in something after all. He realized if he was willing to die then the outcome of the titanic struggle for Zion's survival was a foregone conclusion. The way to peace was in his atoning sacrifice on Zion's behalf. Neo's death was an effective, voluntary, substitutionary death for his race. Sort of like, hmm, er. . . let's see wasn't there someone else who did something like that for the city of Zion? Who *was* that other guy? It's on the tip of my tongue. . . .dang!

Neo realized it didn't matter how many Agent Smiths there were. All that needed to happen was for Neo to face him and allow himself to be killed. As soon as Agent Smith tried to make Neo part of his dark Agent Smith universe, the equilibrium of the real universe would be upset. The equation would no longer be balanced. You can't have yin and yin. You can only have yin and yang.

Neo was no longer plagued with the doubts that were starting to get really boring in the movie. He was "certain" of the victorious outcome. Once he was willing to die at the hands of Agent Smith, he would destroy the Agent Smith in everyone. He had finally become a believer in the prophecies about his own destiny as "The One." The New Man had finally emerged in the person of Keanu Reeves, I mean Neo.

Salvation for the planet lay in the New Man's final recognition of a collision with his own destiny and his willingness to die in order to usher in a New Millennium. The Wachowski brothers would go on to make the movie "V For Vendetta" with another millennial messenger, V, who wore a Guy Fawkes mask. V believed the new Age would come through anarchy. Then he fell in love and found something he was willing to live and die for. Like V, Neo is a type of Jesus, Gandhi, Dr. Martin Luther King, Jr. or any other martyred prophet of a new social order.

Who Offers Real Hope?

Neo is a nice "construct" of philosophy and art on screen, but there is no one in all of real-time human history who fits the Neo prototype or original Superman vision like a no-name Jew from the backwaters of Galilee. All my chips are on Him.

His voice screaming from the cross in an exhausted whisper, "My God, God why have you forsaken me?!" can speak hope to the abused Muslim Palestinian denied every dignity by a system of political "Zionism," hope to the Jew wondering whether they will survive another day in a Nazi death camp or with another Hamas suicide bomber in Israel, hope to the American Indian struggling on a desolate reservation to believe there is a future worth living for, hope to a man or woman tempted to give in to their sexual addictions, hope to the housewife who knows she has never been loved well by her husband, hope for the ambitious Wall Street broker struggling with his lust for money, hope for the mentally and emotionally and physically challenged person tempted to hate themselves, hope. . . for every human being.

I know of no other candidate in human history that I trust more to save us, for real, than this horribly mangled man speaking to God for all of us. He *is* all of us on the cross. In that moment, He is the highest image of what it means to be human and the highest image of what it means to be God. That is why He alone is the God-Man. He is our only intercessor. He alone, became alone, for us.

Jesus shared our dirt nature and died to make it noble once again. We are still waiting for the full promise of a glorious Age to come. But where else can we turn? The Republicans? The Democrats? Any human institution? I am toast if He isn't the One. If Jesus lied or didn't get out of the tomb on Sunday morning, all like me who have hoped in Him for centuries, are the most lost. For me there is no plan B. Hell, if there is a Hell, is where I am heading for believing and spreading such a vicious vanity as hope in Jesus.

Chapter 15

When Doing Good
Isn't Good Enough

"Why do you call me good?" Jesus answered.
"No one is good—except God alone."
(Mark 10:18)

Competing Visions of a New Millennium

The word millennium in Christian thought is both a metaphor and literal word for the ideal reign of God. Our broader society uses the word millennium to refer to any grand future epoch that transcends the age we are in now.

The Wachowski brother's vision of the new social order to come in the *Matrix* Trilogy is obviously a bit different from the one envisioned by the prophets of the 66 Books. But when we are talking about ultimate things, any error in truth is like getting your math wrong when building the St. Louis Gateway Arch. Will all our ideas connect when they reach the top? "Ooops!" is not what you want to say when you see Jesus surfing clouds on his victory laps around the planet.

I respect the honest soul-searching journey that the Wachowski brothers are on. They are amazing artists and they have some of the millennial vision right. The love of Trinity and (her) willingness to go all the way is what inspires us, like Neo, to lay down our own lives in love for others. For the Wachowskis, sacrificial love for human beings is the highest value in a dark universe. Compassion, self-sacrifice, and love for others are truly noble values.

Hollywood has discovered you can still make a lot of money producing movies with that message. I am glad for that. Jesus modeled these values more than any human being who ever lived. But lest we think that love for others is the pinnacle of noble existence, I must remind myself and you that in biblical terms, love for others is the *second* great commandment. The first and greatest reason we exist at all is to return the affections of our Father God. He loves us with all His heart, mind, soul, and strength, and longs to receive our matched affections back.

I remember telling my wife when we were dating that I love her best when I love God most. Love for God is the wellspring of love for others. When first commandment love dries up, love for others is not far behind.

Altruism is Not Enough

There is more to solving the human enigma than us loving each other. Altruism, or the willingness to sacrifice oneself in love for others, while noble, is not enough to save us.

The unresolved part of the *Matrix* equation is the part J.R.R. Tolkien got right in his great work of literary art, *The Lord of the Rings*. The *more* that is essential to resolving our broken human psyche goes far beyond mere humanitarian altruism. The real key to solving the *Matrix* and understanding the *Lord of the Rings* Trilogy is that there is a "right to our worship" exclusively due to the One Real God. Tolkien wrote this in one of his letters to a friend, "In the Lord of the Rings the conflict is not basically about freedom, though that is naturally involved. It is about God, and His sole right to divine honor" (*The Letters of J. R. R. Tolkien*, 243).

Tolkien believed in a literal thousand year future earthly government by Jesus with His saints, which is unusual for a Roman Catholic like himself (110). Perhaps, the title of the third book is not called *The Return of the King* by accident. We'll get to Tolkien later. But first we need to go deeper into the Bridal Covenant God made with Israel at Sinai. Specifically, we need to gaze at the "Ten Commandments" summary of the Mosaic Law.

Four Plus Six Equals Two

The first four of the Ten Commandments at Sinai were about loving God foremost. He wants all of our love, not just some. God wants us to love Him with "all our heart, mind, soul, and strength" because He loves us with all *His* heart, mind, soul, and strength. Fair enough!

Modern artists and politicians in Western Civilization are growing more sensitive to "human rights," but more deaf to any notion that God also has "rights." In fact, God is the *only* person with true rights. Jesus is *entitled* to our worship, but He woos us with Bridal affections, because He wants to be wanted. Who wouldn't? Lovers want *voluntary* matched affections.

When asked by a young, up and coming "Wall Street" broker, "How can I get to Heaven?" Jesus told him in Mark Chapter Ten to sell his portfolio and give the whole enchilada to the poor. His investment would be safe in Heaven. Then he could jump in with Jesus' crew and let the fun begin!

The broker didn't see it as a good deal and walked away bummed. I bet if that man could advise any of us investors today from where he is now, he would be shouting, "Sell! Sell!" No matter how things appear, from the eternal perspective, God never asks us to trade down.

When Jesus answered the Wall Street broker, He reminded this good church-goer of the last six of the Ten Commands God gave Moses for the Bridal Ceremony. The religious young man said, "I have done all six of those."

Then Jesus said, "Okay. This is what you lack." That is when He invited this precious man to trade up his portfolio. But what was it he *really* lacked? The broker lacked obedience to the first four commandments about wholehearted love for God. He lacked *intimacy* with the One who knew and loved him most.

Jesus simplified the Ten Commandments into Two Commandments in Matthew 22:37-40. The first and greatest commandment Jesus said is "Love the Lord your God with all your heart, all your soul, and all your mind. The second commandment is like it, love others as you love yourself."

Ten Commandments are condensed into two.

1) Love God (Commands 1 to 4)
2) Love others as you would yourself (Commands 5 to 10) Four plus Six equals two!

Most of us grade ourselves well on the human relationship part of Jesus' second commandment. But, like the rich young broker, we aren't remotely in touch with our lack of love for God. The fourth of the Ten Commandments is really about spending quality time with our Heavenly Father. We know it as keeping "Sabbath." One out of every seven days is reserved for special hang out time with Him. He is worth it, right? So when was the last time you took a whole day to be still and love on God?

Six Commandments for Human Relationships

The last six commandments are dear to God as well. Loving others is part of loving Him. Let's look at the six requirements about loving other people from God's perspective.

Honor Mom and Dad. No matter how they act, I chose them for you. You aren't you, apart from them. Figure out, with My help, what honoring them looks like. It can be okay to keep a safe distance, just don't disengage long term. You'll be amazed in the end how much better your life will go if you stay connected to your legacy. I *know* it can be hard sometimes. Why do you think I made this a core value in my covenant with you?

Don't murder people. That includes little ones in the womb and big ones outside the womb that I made in my image. They may not look, act, smell, sound like you, or like the same movies, but I am a Potter who shapes clay as it seems best to Me. I like variety, so learn to like how I made *all* my children. They are your brothers and sisters.

Don't cheat on the one you promised never to cheat on – your covenant partner in marriage. I am a promise keeper and I want everyone who claims to know Me to keep their promises, too. I will help you keep your promises, if you ask Me. You said you loved them once. Now prove it.

Don't steal stuff. I am watching your life and I expect honesty. That means you don't take anything that doesn't belong to you. Remember, just because it doesn't appear that anybody is looking, I have microphones under every ash tray. The CIA can't touch my surveillance ability. I have everything on DVD from every angle, so don't even think about making stupid alibis, which leads me to the next requirement.

Don't lie on each other. You may pull the wool over Judge Judy or some other Court Room Judge, but I am waiting to bust you big time if you think you are getting away with not telling the whole truth. Better to tell it all now and face the consequences than try to change the story to benefit yourself or the people waiting to slip you something outside the court room; if they haven't stuffed your pocket already.

Don't give in to jealousy and greed. So what if your neighbor's wife has kept her figure into her late forties? She isn't the one you made a promise to. She isn't the mother of your children. Stop fantasizing about ways to get her in bed. So what if Rev. Jones has a more attention-getting ministry than yours. Don't figure out a way to take it away or undermine it with slick spiritual sounding language. That is only greed with a pious wrapping. It is how Satan convinced Cain to kill Abel. Plow your own field and bring Me worship from your own hands. I don't care about the size of the field. I care about the worship of your heart.

By the way, My friend, King David, broke all Ten of My laws at once. He dishonored Me and his parents when he coveted Uriah's wife and committed adultery with her. This happened during a period of Sabbath rest from fighting wars. Instead of hanging out with Me down at the place where the singers and worshippers were gazing at my beauty over the Ark, David preferred the beauty of Bathsheba. She became an idol to him. He abused the authority I gave him to have Uriah murdered and cover up His utter contempt for me and others. If I can restore David, I can forgive and restore you.

David deserved judgment, but got mercy. Why? Read Psalm 51. It is his song of brokenness and confession after he got busted by God's prophet, Nathan. God will *never* refuse a humble heart crying for mercy. Because David was a man after God's heart of mercy he finished life well in spite of many failings.

Happy Endings

Like any story, the *Matrix* Trilogy had to end sometime. I doubt Christian movie makers could have made a more biblical ending for Matrix Revolutions. Neo's atoning sacrifice brought a happy ending to a sad era of human history and opened up a glorious millennium for the City of Zion.

In the final scene, the Oracle and the little Indian girl gaze on a beautiful celestial city with a glorious light shining out of it. They anticipate seeing Neo again there somehow. You can't tell me the Wachowski brothers didn't have their finger in the last chapter of Revelation when they made that scene.

No longer will there be any curse. The throne of God and of the Lamb will be in the city, and His servants will serve Him. They will see His face and His Name will be on their foreheads. There will be no more night. They will not need the light of a lamp or the light of the sun, for the Lord God will give them light. And they will reign forever and ever. (Rev. 22:3-5)

Only one man has lived a life perfectly pleasing to God. Because Jesus has already finished life triumphantly, all who trust in His leadership also finish life and history well. Our goodness will never be enough to save us, but His goodness already has.

Chapter 16

Will the Real Superman Stand Up?

Jesus and his disciples went on to the villages
around Caesarea Philippi.
On the way he asked them, "Who do people say I am?"
They replied, "Some say John the Baptist; others say Elijah;
and still others, one of the prophets."
"But what about you?" he asked. "Who do you say I am?"
Peter answered, "You are the Christ."
(Mark 8:27-29)

The Original Superman

Nietzsche was right. It would take a Neo-like Superman to change the world. What Nietzsche missed is what kind of Superman it would take. Nietzsche wrote off Jesus.

A few years before Nietzsche, another genius wrote about the "Ubermensch" idea. It was a gambling addicted novelist named Fyodor Dostoyevsky. Dostoyevsky wrote some amazing books that took his Russian Czarist dominated world by storm. He also made millions of American high school students taking world literature long after his death very unhappy.

I admit that his 1866 novel, *Crime and Punishment*, was totally wasted on me in high school. I didn't discover the amazing genius of Dostoyevsky until after discovering Jesus. In some ways, it is impossible to understand any of Dostoyevsky's novels without first understanding the Jesus he knew.

Dostoyevsky wrote in a time when the idea of a "Great Man" or second Napoleon was very intriguing to intellectuals and politicians in Europe. To Dostoyevsky the notion was a disaster waiting to happen. Just as the French had cast off the corrupt and obsolete influence of the Roman Catholic supported French monarchy in favor of a libertarian secular democracy about eighty years before, the Russian people were tiring of their failed monarchy crowned by the Russian Orthodox Church.

Dostoyevsky's novels were read in Soviet Russia long after the Communists had banned the 66 Books. His prophetic insight into the convoluted human psyche was the *Matrix* Trilogy of his day. He plumbed the depths of both the human soul and the heart of darkness in mankind.

His genius for social critique laid bare not only the ludicrous notion of the State serving as "Ubermensch," but he also used the scalpel of his art on the corrupt institution of the Church. To this day, the chapter in *The Brothers Karamasov* called "The Grand Inquisitor" stands as a testimony against any form of Christianity that profits from the high moral vision and life of Jesus without actually following Him.

Because of the depth of our depravity as sons and daughters of God, we will pervert "truth" for our own version of the Millennial Reign. As soon as Christianity became a political asset, it was quickly co-opted by the "principalities and powers" to serve an age old earthly kingdom run by the Dark Prince of this Age.

Do We Live in a Moral Universe or Not?

In *Crime and Punishment*, a young man experiments with the idea that he might be a Superman. The Superman would be able to transcend the false moral boundaries supported by outdated ideas of man and religion. So to test the theory, Raskolnikov, murders an old woman in his apartments and covers up his crime. The rest of the novel is the tale of Raskolnikov's tortured psyche as Porfiry the Sheriff dabbles with the clues surrounding Raskolnikov's guilt.

Porfiry never nails Raskolnikov, but he doesn't have to. God does. Or should we say, God working through his tortured conscience and the faith in Christ of a woman named Sonia. She is a mother forced into prostitution to care for her child. The climax of the story is when Raskolnikov realizes that he *does* live in a moral universe. One human being cannot assert their will on another human being and not pay the consequences. There is a God of Heaven and Earth who sees all and will judge everyone in the Person of Jesus.

Dostoyevsky is warning his generation, "If you have any sense at all, make your peace with Jesus now, before it is too late." Sadly his warning didn't keep totalitarian Communism from replacing totalitarian Czarism. Will Democracy and Free Market ideas save the Russian soul today? Have they saved the American soul? No.

I have stood in the square in St. Petersburg, Russia where Raskolnikov threw himself to the pavement in wracking repentance in the novel. His soul was not free, nor his conscience clear, until he confessed his crime to God. Turning himself in to Porfiry to receive just punishment for his crime was a piece of cake after that.

We Can't Let Go of Superman

Those who have found their search for Neo in a carpenter's son from Smallsville know something Nietzsche never learned. Agape love is stronger than life and death. . .and world politics.

So why has most of the world today given up on the idea that Jesus is not just the theological answer to the world's problem, He is the *political* answer to the world's problem? Partly because we think theology only has to do with "pie in the sky" and politics is about "I want my pie now." Or for some of us who already have our pie. "I want *more* pie in *this* flavor." We will follow the leader who can give us the biggest slice of the pie now. It matters little if it is a monarchy, dictatorship, federal democracy, or Islamic State, we will follow the person or system that promises *us* the best future. Is that wrong? Maybe. Maybe not. Who is your Superman?

Jesus and Swiper Square Off

All of our philosophic pontifications go out the window when we are facing the full authority of a spiritual "principality." That is when we fly our "true colors" or core values. It is called a "power encounter" by some. They are the defining moments in life.

It is interesting that the first thing that God directs Jesus to do after Cousin John dips Jesus in the Jordan River is to go hang out in the desert without food for 40 days before meeting the "Prince of This World."

The Prince of Peace is ready to "get this show on the road," but the first stop is a barren wilderness to go head to head with the Prince of Darkness. It should tip us off that job one for Jesus' first mission to Planet Earth is to settle the old score with "Swiper."

If you have never seen Dora the Explorer, then you don't know what I mean! It is a kids' show on Public Television and there is a character named Swiper who is always trying to swipe things from a little girl named Dora. Once uncovered, he really is no big deal. He is told, "Now Swiper, no more swiping!" He says, "Oh man!" and has to walk away.

Jesus has come to tell Swiper to stop swiping. Swiper, or Satan in this case, *is* a big deal. We are no match for him without Jesus backing us up. Satan has real authority because we sold our inheritance to him in the Garden by choosing his word over Dad's. He has temporary, but real, authority to govern this world that God first gave to us.

Hear what Swiper tells Jesus during the second of the three tests at the end of the 40 day fast:

The Devil led Him up to a high place and showed Him in an instant all the kingdoms of the world. And he said to Him, "I will give You all their authority and splendor, for it has been given to me, and I can give it to anyone I want to. So if you worship me, it will all be yours." (Luke 4:5-7)

All authority is established by God. We are commanded by Paul to pray for *all* those in authority. This is the same guy who had his head chopped off by the Roman government, so I think Paul was willing to live by that statement. He wasn't just saying pray for "good" governments. The only thing worse than an evil government is no government at all. The first thing God does is establish authority. He ordered Creation by fiat, His own word, then He put Adam in charge of it. God delegated government to Man and Woman as vice-regents in the Garden. We gave it away to Swiper and Jesus is getting it back for us.

If you are like me, you might ask, "Why does God's plan to buy everything back that was stolen involve so much pain and suffering?" Because of how profoundly deep the tear of our sin is in God's order, He cannot simply snap his fingers, or wiggle his celestial nose to make everything better. The redemption of a race of sinners includes very great and very real suffering. The 66 Books does not side step pain. Like John the Baptist and Paul the Apostle, the good guys get their heads handed over to God's enemies. . . for little while.

It was granted to him (Satan) to make war with the saints and to overcome them. And authority was given him over every tribe, tongue, and nation. All who dwell on the earth will worship him, whose names have not been written in the Book of Life of the Lamb who was slain from the foundation of the world (Rev. 13:7-8)

One thing about the Bible—it doesn't sugar-coat bad news. God tells His own kids that He is going to let our Enemy kick our tails. I really wish it didn't work that way. . . and yet. Maybe there is something so much better that happens when we keep taking that next faithful step on our own Way of the Cross. Satan "overcame" Jesus on the cross. But it was his worst idea ever.

The cosmic conflict, manifested through world politics, has everything to do with worship. The one who is on the highest throne has the "right" to receive worship. Millions of people that God esteems from Heaven are walking the Earth right now. We don't really see each other accurately because our value system is still so tainted by the charisma of the world. But one day, to the shock of kings and celebrities, the real outcome of the war of the cosmos will be made obvious to all. The issue is being decided right now inside of every human heart. Inside of *your* heart.

Will you be among the shining ones who died without fanfare, standing as a trophy of God's grace? Will you be a part of the ones seen by God and hated by the Devil? Can you say to Jesus in your deepest heart today, "Your love is *better* than life."

Lord of the Rings

J.R.R. Tolkien's *Lord of the Rings* fantasy novel trilogy adapted into a movie trilogy has also made the cultural icon Hall of Fame. I have no idea what movie director Peter Jackson's world view is, but he sure can create an awesome world of Middle Earth! He succeeded in living up to our high expectations for depicting on-screen Tolkien's literary masterpiece of fantasy fiction.

Ever since *The Lord of the Rings* fantasy epic became a box office phenomenon, there have been quickly written fantasy genre knockoffs, some with anti-biblical messages displayed with the same breathtaking special effects. But none of the fantasy successors can top a little hobbit ending the argument over who will take the Ring of Power on an impossible quest to destroy it in Tolkien's version of Hell. Frodo sums up the invitation of Jesus Himself to take up our cross and follow Him when the hobbit says to representatives of Middle Earth, "I will take the ring!. . . though I do not know the way."

What many lovers of the fantasy genre may *not* know, is that Tolkien's world view was based on the Bible. Tolkien was a part of a small group of cigar smoking, beer sipping Oxford thinkers and writers who called themselves the "Inklings." C.S. Lewis of Narnia fame and J.R.R. Tolkien were among them. I guess you had to go by your initials to sit at their table.

Besides their enjoyment of English pubs while discussing long thoughts, they were followers of Jesus. Anything you ever wanted to know about what J.R.R. really thought you can find in the book, *The Letters of J.R.R. Tolkien.* Remember the quote earlier in this book about Tolkien's view of conflict in his brain-child? "In the Lord of the Rings the conflict is not basically about freedom, though that is naturally involved. It is about God, and His sole right to divine honor" (243).

Wow. You are pardoned if you didn't discern that meaning in your actual reading of the trilogy. It isn't as clear in the novel as Tolkien puts it in his letter. But there you have what the author himself says about what all the fuss is about. Who, at the end of the day, has the right to be worshipped?

Like the Wachowski brothers of *Matrix* fame, film director Peter Jackson ends his movie trilogy by ripping the last page of the Bible out and pasting it in his anticlimax. Well, forget about the long Hobbit goodbyes at the end. What I mean is, Aragorn, like Jesus, is finally revealed as the true heir to the throne in a New Millennial Kingdom. Sauron's dark kingdom, like Satan's, and his grip over Middle Earth, is broken. The wedding of Aragorn and Arwin as the New Age begins, smacks of Jesus and His Bride, the Church, at His return as the Bridegroom King. Minas Tirith is a type of New Jerusalem.

The Age of a Redeemed Humanity dawned in Middle Earth. But *we* aren't there yet. The worship war is still raging here on regular earth. Jesus, the real Superman has many imitators.

The last Anti-Superman is yet to be revealed.

Chapter 17

The Invisible War

(The angelic messenger said) "Do not be afraid, Daniel. Since the first day that you set your mind to gain understanding and to humble yourself before your God, your words were heard, and I have come in response to them. But the prince of the Persian kingdom resisted me twenty-one days."
(Daniel 10:12)

Spiritual War in Heaven Lands on the Earth

In the description of the Millennium in Revelation, Satan is bound and kept in a prison called the Abyss until the end of the thousand years.

And I saw an angel coming down out of heaven, having the key to the Abyss and holding in his hand a great chain. He seized the dragon, that ancient serpent, who is the devil, or Satan, and bound him for a thousand years. He threw him into the Abyss, and locked and sealed it over him, to keep him from deceiving the nations anymore until the thousand years were ended. After that, he must be set free for a short time. (Rev. 20:1-3)

A Premillennialist reading of this passage sees the Millennium coming after the return of Christ. Jesus triumphed over the dark powers at the cross (Col.2:15), but Satan is still actively deceiving the nations. The cross is like the D-Day invasion of WWII, a decisive battle won making victory sure, but the war is not over. Satan and dark powers are doomed but not yet imprisoned in the Abyss.

Amillennialists believe we are currently in the Millennium. If Satan is bound in the Abyss during the Millennium, *in what way* is he bound since there are so many post-ascension references to him? (i.e., Jesus in Acts 26:16, Rev. 2:9, 2:13, 2:24, and 3:9. Peter in Acts 5:3 and 1 Peter 5:8. James in James 4:7. Paul has references in six of his letters. John in 1 John 3:8-10.)

Let's look Ephesians 2:1-2, 6-7 through an Amillennial lens:

*As for you, you were dead in your transgressions and sins, in which you used to live when you followed the ways of this world and of **the ruler of the kingdom of the air, the spirit who is now at work in those who are disobedient**. . . And God raised us up with Christ and seated us with him in the heavenly realms in Christ Jesus, in order that in the coming ages he might show the incomparable riches of his grace, expressed in his kindness to us in Christ Jesus.*

The idea here is that Satan is bound from destroying the church which is seated with Christ, though he is still at work in the world through the unredeemed. However, in Revelation 20, Satan is bound from deceiving the nations not just bound from deceiving the church.

If we are not yet in the Millennial Kingdom of Revelation 20, there is a very real spiritual war going on right now that includes angels and demons. The Praying Church is the way Jesus is currently ruling in the midst of His enemies.

Then another sign appeared in heaven; an enormous red dragon with seven heads and ten horns and seven crowns on his heads. His tail swept a third of the stars out of the sky and flung them to the earth. And there was war in heaven. Michael and his angels fought back. But he was not strong enough, and they lost their place in heaven. The great dragon was hurled down – that ancient serpent called the devil, or Satan, who leads the whole world astray. He was hurled to the earth and his angels with him. Woe to the earth and the sea, because the devil has gone down to you! He is filled with fury, because he knows that his time is short. (Rev. 12:3,4,7-9, 12)

Demonic forces are a part of the equation of our human history. They are ordered in ranks; new levels, new devils. We forget they are around. That suits them just fine.

For our struggle is not against flesh and blood, but against the rulers, against the authorities, against the powers of this dark world and against the spiritual forces of evil in the heavenly realms. (Ephesians 6:12)

The battle is for human hearts across the whole planet. Who, or what, is worthy of our highest affections? The fuss over worship is not about head knowledge of God or about Rambo-like spiritual warfare tactics, but about intimacy between our hearts and Jesus. It is an all out 24/7 war. Right beliefs are vital, but if we have right theology and smoking miracle pistols without a deep abiding relationship with God, we are easy prey for Swiper and his crew. "Knowledge puffs up, but love builds up" (1 Cor. 8:1).

There are three arenas that make up the triad of right living. They cannot be separated. Orthodoxy is "right thinking." Orthopraxis is "right action." Orthopathos is "right emotions." They make up what we call the "soul." The soul is the seat of the Mind, Will, and Emotions. While all three are essential, the final battle will be over the affections of the hearts of women and men. "Because of the increase of wickedness, the *love* of most will grow cold, but he who stands firm to the end will be saved" (Matthew 24:12-13). The evidence of a saved soul is perseverance in love for Jesus.

Jesus asked, "When the Son of Man returns, will He find faith on the earth?" (Luke 18:8). He wasn't talking about faith as right information. He didn't only die for seminary students. It was the seminarians of Israel giving Him the most grief! He was talking about a fiery devotion and agreement in the heart of His Bride.

I wonder if the above question of Jesus is a prayer? "Father, will My Bride persevere in faith, hope, and love? Will She wait for Me and not give Herself to other lovers? Will She remain tender toward Her enemies, even as She is being falsely accused and killed? Will She become more like I became in my last hour? I love the questions and longings in Jesus prayers! They awaken love in my heart back to Him.

There is a Louder Shout to Come

I believe the greatest generation of Jesus lovers is still in front of us. Lucy and I are preparing our family to be among them. The finest hour of the Bridal People will be the hour before His shout is heard from pole to pole. The Bride of Jesus is most radiant, not when she is the most materially or politically prosperous, but when she loves Him under the most spiritual pressure.

The real battle isn't over who *gets* the most, it is over who *loves* the most. Jesus already has it all! If I had a choice between what Warren Buffett has now, and receiving from Jesus later. Phewwww. What choice?

Just like Swiper offered Jesus the world, he tempts each of us as well. Don't fall for his old tricks. Even though he can use the Bible better than Louis Farrakhan, the Wachowskis, or your Humanities professor put together, the Holy Spirit will bring to your mind the Word of God to overcome Swiper. Give yourself to knowing Scripture so the Holy Spirit has more to work with!

Jesus was physically spent when Swiper came to Him in the desert. But His grasp of truth and love for His Father enabled Him to overcome temptation. The wilderness confrontation was boot camp for the cross.

I often ask Lucy or my boys this question: "Who loves you?" I love the confident answer they give me. "You do!" There are a lot of things Swiper can do. He can offer pretty cool stuff. But one thing Swiper will never do. He will never lay down his life for you in love. It ain't happenin'. He is *not* a good Husband, good Friend, or good Dad. Jesus said, "The Devil comes to steal, kill, and destroy. I have come that you may have life, life to the fullest!" (John 10:10)

Jesus bet the whole enterprise, like Neo, on one outcome with His own blood. Hanging from the tree He asks, "Who loves you?"

How will you respond? Who will you give your love to? For me, it's the one who loves me the most and who offers his leadership not only in this present Age, but in the Age to come. He gets my worship. But that doesn't mean Swiper is done with me yet.

Swiper's Hit-Man

Sauron had Saruman in *Lord of the Rings*. The machines had Agent Smith in the *Matrix*. Satan is going to have a human being who rises to power in some form of global influence. Many have speculated as to his identity over the centuries. He is known in the Bible as the "Anti-Christ" or "Man of Perdition." He will be the "Ubermensch" humanity turns to at the end of the Age to get us out of the mess all our collective sin got us into. He will be *us*, our fleshly us, on steroids. Just as Jesus is all of us at our most vulnerable and self-giving, the Anti-Jesus will be all of us at our most power wielding and self infatuated.

Counterfeit miracles? No problem. The Dark Kingdom has that power as the two magicians of Pharoah, Jannes and Jambres, proved to Moses thousands of years ago. God turned Moses' staff into a snake. Then J and J turned their staffs into snakes. Then Moses' snake ate both of theirs. Now that is pretty cool! It was sort of the original Pokemon battle.

The coming of the Man of Perdition will be in accordance with the work of Satan displayed in all kinds of counterfeit miracles, signs, and wonders, and in every sort of evil that deceives those who are perishing. They perish because they refused to love the truth and so be saved. For this reason God sends them a powerful delusion so that they believe the lie and so that all will be condemned who have not believed the truth, but have delighted in wickedness. (2 Thess. 2:9-11)

The first generation of Jesus followers was taught of a future Anti-Christ. The concept is a part of historic Christianity even if it is rarely mentioned in some churches. All the early Church fathers who wrote about the Anti-Christ believed he was a real person to be revealed in the future. Those today with the Preterist view who believe that the Roman Emperor Nero in the 60s AD was the total fulfillment of the Anti-Christ prophecies have to explain how all of the early Church fathers failed to correctly interpret the apostles on that point.

Because there is confusion around the subject of the Anti-Christ, many pastors are reluctant to teach about it. To prepare for the leadership of Jesus means we must also prepare for the leadership of the Anti-Jesus. He is still to come, too. We better talk about him. History is full of "Anti-Messianic forerunners" who made their move when conditions swung their way.

Hitler persuaded a "Christian" German population to arise as a superior Aryan Race to conquer the world and exterminate Jews. He never performed a miracle.

Muhammad expected the Jewish tribes of Arabia to receive him as a prophet of God in the early 600s. When they did not, he massacred them. He never claimed to have performed a miracle, though Muslims would say that the Qu'ran itself is a miracle. I love Muslim people. But the part we disagree upon happens to be the most important one. Muhammad teaches that Jesus did not die on the cross to cover our sin with His blood. That one point negates the whole of meaningful Christianity.

The Spirit of Anti-Messiah was operating in the Roman and Jewish rulers when they conspired to nail Jesus to a cross. The High Priest Caiaphas reasoned that it was better that one man should die than for the whole nation to be misled. Jesus was an enemy of the Jewish State.

Jesus warned his closest followers, "They will put you out of the synagogue; in fact *a time is coming when anyone who kills you will think he is offering a service to God*" (John 16:2). Jesus knew what his closest friends were in for. He was preparing them to suffer well. Are we preparing our sons and daughters to live well in the Age to come, or are we only preparing them for the passing "American Dream" and unwittingly setting them up for the leadership of the Anti-Christ?

Money, Money, Money, Money

Swiper often sends his lieutenants to operate the deception, death, and false worship campaign. One is Mammon. He is the guy who makes people cry on game shows. He isn't the Anti-Christ, but he is one of the antichrist spirits. His name can be translated "Money." Jesus said, "You cannot serve both God and Money. You will end up loving one and hating the other." Yikes! Money isn't just some theory that put me to sleep as a college freshman reading Macroeconomics. According to Jesus, Money is a Dark Prince.

Some television preachers instruct their flock to call out "Money, come to me!" Whoa. You might want to remember what Paul said about lovers of Money before you invite him into your life:

But those who desire to be rich fall into temptation, into a snare, into many senseless and hurtful desires that plunge men into ruin and destruction. For the love of money is the root of all evils. It is through this craving that some have wandered away from the faith and pierced their hearts with many pangs. (1 Tim. 6:9-10)

Flip Wilson was a comedian in the 1970s. He played characters, like "Geraldine," who had a boyfriend named "Killah." They used to sit "in-the-booth-in-the-back-in-the-corner-in-the-dark." Another character was the preacher of "The Church of What's Happenin' Now." He would strut out to the Pink Floyd tune, "Money, money, money, money. . .Money!" He said in one sermon, "Many of you have asked, 'Why don't you sell one of your diamond rings and give it to the poor, or give away one of your Cadillacs, or one of your boats? That's *easy* for you to say. You *have* none of these things!'"

Money is a great servant but a terrible master. Listen to what we say about Mr. Money in our culture. "He makes the world go around." "He talks and people listen." "Follow the Money (him)." "Show me the Money." "You can't do anything without (him)." "Money is power."

Maybe Jesus had a point about this guy? He sounds like a pretty deceptive and powerful competitor for our worship. He even has folk preaching his lordship in some of our churches.

Jacques Ellul, a French intellectual wrote, "The love of money is always the sign of another need – to protect oneself, to be a superman, for survival, or for eternity. And what better means to attain all this than wealth? In our frantic breathless search we are not looking for entertainment alone. *We are looking, without realizing it for eternity.* Now money does not satisfy our hunger nor respond to our love. We are on the wrong road. We have used the wrong means" (*Money and Power*, IVP, 54).

Open the Case

It is hard not to get engrossed in the drama of whether there is a gob of life altering cash in the case on "Deal or No Deal." I think a lot about money. We all do. More than we like to admit. It is *how* we think about it that matters.

Jesus talked a surprising amount about money in the New Testament. Jesus is eager to converse about our relationship with the resources He has entrusted to us and our stewardship of it. It is one of those things we will give an account for when stand before Him.

He wants the Bridal People to be very wise in their use of wealth because we will have an insane amount of true riches in the Age to come. He doesn't want idiots managing the planets portfolio in His Millennial Reign. He promoted people in the Bible, like Joseph and Daniel, in order to show that wise government over resources is a good thing. We are to use money to please God instead of using God to please Money.

Old Game – New Tricks

Swiper only has three real cards to play. Money, Sex, and Power. You can argue there are more cards, like security, death, false religion, and well, baseball cards if that is your weak spot. But for the sake of simplicity, let's go with Money, Sex, and Power and say others are variations on the theme.

Do not love the world or the things of the world. If anyone loves the world, love for the Father is not in him. For all that is in the world, the lust of the flesh, the lust of the eyes, and the pride of life, is not of the Father, but is of the world which is passing away and the lust of it; but he who does the will of God abides forever. Children, it is the last hour; and as you have heard that Antichrist is coming, so now many antichrists have come; therefore we know that it is the last hour. (1 John 2:15-18)

John says the Anti-Christ is coming but that many types of anti-christ, like the Spirit of Mammon, have already come. Swiper isn't choosy about which Anti-Christ spirit he uses to keep us in his grip. If lust of the flesh is our poison of choice. . . works for him! If the cravings of our eyes keep us as grounded eagles. . . cha-ching. If we never see past our own pride. . . we aren't even making him sweat. His schemes don't have to be anything more elaborate than blind ambition or selfish addictions. The system of the world works externally alongside our fleshly desires and to keep us happily dreaming away in Swiper's Kingdom like the human batteries in the *Matrix*.

Whose Voice Are We Listening To?

It is vital to keeping the right pair of earphones on as you read the Bible. God's requirements can sound more like a reactionary Father than a Jealous Bridegroom. Depending on our own life story, we may respond differently to one voice than the other. As our Father, God can get angry. That counts. We need to hear that voice and respond well. "Those whom I love, I rebuke and discipline. So be earnest and repent" (Rev. 3:19). As our Lover, our Bridegroom can be angry when we cheat on Him. That counts, too. God has emotions and we need to turn to His voice when He is warning us.

Since Swiper can misquote the Bible to us, we need to know the "voice" of the Author. We need to hear the One whose voice is described in Solomon's Song of Songs.

The voice of my Beloved! Behold He comes, leaping upon the mountains, bounding over the hills. My Beloved is like a gazelle, or young stag. Behold, there He stands, behind our wall, gazing in at the windows, looking through the lattice. My Beloved speaks and says to me: 'Arise, my love, my fair one, and come away. . .let Me see your *face, let me hear your voice, for your voice is sweet, and your face* *is comely.* (Song of Songs 2:8-10,14)

To hear the voice of Jesus is every believer's inheritance. "My sheep hear my voice, but a stranger they will not follow" (John 10:4-5). He is for us, not against us. His should be the voice behind us that whispers right directions. Don't let Swiper stand behind you whispering in your ear. That is Dad's place.

Our own unredeemed minds, the world, and the Devil have their own counterfeit voice. The best way to spot a counterfeit is to know the genuine article front and back. Instead of becoming paranoid about deciphering every Anti-Christ possibility, we ought to simply give ourselves to a deep life of intimacy with the Christ Himself. Then anything or anyone who doesn't look, smell, sound, act, love, or live like Him, we can pass by.

Beloved, do not believe every spirit, but test the spirits to see whether *they are of God; for many false prophets have gone out into the* *world. By this you know the Spirit of God; every spirit which con-* *fesses that Jesus Christ has come in the flesh is of God, and every* *spirit which does not confess Jesus is not of God. This is the spirit* *of antichrist, of which you heard that it was coming, and now it is* *in the world already. Little children, you are of God and have over-* *come them; for He who is in you is greater than he who is in the* *world.* (I John 4:1-4)

The best defense against the Anti-Christ spirit is simply to go on being filled with the love and truth of God. Those who abide in the love of Jesus have nothing to fear. *"There is no fear in love, but* *perfect love casts out fear, for fear has to do with punishment. . . We* *love because He first loved us"* (1 John 4:18-19).

A Fight to the Finish

There is a battle of messengers throughout history. The battle is over the future and who it belongs to. Artists, writers, politicians, philosophers, religionists, and revolutionaries in every generation have attempted to promote their own brand of the future. We must discern the voices in our generation. The Bible states the battle is between the influence of the Dark Powers of this Age or Jesus of Nazareth who brings an Age to come. Crazy, huh? But there it is.

Satan will throw everything, including the kitchen sink, at those longing for the leadership of Jesus. He knows his time is short and he is crafty. Satan will have his own man in charge of the whole earth for a few years. Global crisis will open the door for this man who will be revealed as the Anti-Messiah after he is in power. That won't keep most of the world from following him.

The best recent example of one who discerned the rise of an Anti-Christ leader in his generation is Dietrich Bonhoeffer, the German pastor and theologian. Eric Metaxis' excellent biography, *Bonhoeffer*, details how he stood against the rise of Adolf Hitler and the Third Reich of Germany. Bonhoeffer died by execution in the Flossenberg concentration camp at Hitler's personal directive just weeks before the end of the World War II in Europe.

Like the nominally religious Germans of Hitler's day, those who only give lip service to belonging to Jesus will be easily misled by the future Anti-Christ. We need to beware of the twisted logic and cold love of current peddlers of faith, money, false religions, false empires, and false futures. If we live for this Age only, we will perish with it. What is all the fuss about? It is about who, or what, deserves our worship. It is a battle of millennial messengers. It is a fight to the finish.

Chapter 18

The Sign of the Temple

*Jesus left the temple and was walking away
when his disciples came up to him to call his
attention to its buildings.*
*"Do you see all these things?" he asked. "I tell you the truth,
not one stone here will be left on another;
every one will be thrown down."*
*As Jesus was sitting on the Mount of Olives, the disciples came to
him privately. "Tell us," they said, "when will this happen, and
what will be the sign of your coming and of the end of the age?"*
(Matthew 24:1-3)

Will there be a Third Jewish Temple in Jerusalem?

I am humbly aware of the history of failed speculations resulting from premature attempts to reconcile biblical prophecy with current events. So here is my disclaimer. My thoughts are not a prophecy but a scenario that I hope is plausible enough to spark further prayer and discussion. If there is to be a Third Jerusalem Temple it will not offer an alternative means of God's salvation. The New Testament is clear that the death of Jesus brought full and final redemption for the sins of all who trust Him. All Jews need Jesus today just as much as everyone else. The Temple system with its animal sacrifices became obsolete when Jesus was raised from the dead. There is no going back.

So, if the full and final atoning sacrifice of Jesus on the cross made the whole Mosaic Temple system obsolete, why would God allow an obsolete system to re-emerge if only for a short time before Jesus returns as the Messiah King?

I see two reasons:

1) To fulfill remaining Biblical prophecy.

There is a case that a rebuilt Jewish temple in the city of Jerusalem is a pre-cursor to the return of Jesus. One interpretation of Daniel 9:27 is the Anti-Christ Ruler will engineer a peace treaty with Israel, but then break it in the middle of a seven year countdown prior to the return of Christ. The Anti-Christ Ruler will set up an "abomination that causes desolation" in the temple that launches the three and a half year Great Tribulation period as predicted in the book of Daniel (Daniel 9:27, 11:31, and 12:11) and repeated by Jesus (Matt 24:15). If the abomination of desolation refers *only* to how the Romans defiled the Temple before destroying it in 70 AD, then one reason for a third Temple is moot.

However, in both Daniel's and Jesus' prophecies, the context of the abomination that causes desolation appearing in the Temple includes intertwined references to the final climactic moment of history. Jesus' prophecy has a "near and far" element to it. Those who believe a Millennial Kingdom is coming on the earth view Matthew 24:15-35 as only partially fulfilled in 70 AD. Another Temple is needed to fulfill prophecy that the Anti-Christ will put an end to sacrifices and defile the Temple three and one half years before the return of Jesus.

Don't let anyone deceive you in any way, for (that day will not come) until the rebellion occurs and the man of lawlessness is revealed, the man doomed to destruction. He will oppose and will exalt himself over everything that is called God or is worshiped, so that he sets himself up in God's temple, proclaiming himself to be God. (2 Thess. 2:3,4)

This passage about the return of Jesus is written by Paul before the Second Temple is destroyed. Christians with a Preterist view argue for fulfillment of this prophecy in the first century when the Romans defiled the Jewish Temple before destroying it. But since the Anti- Christ is seen by church fathers in later centuries as still coming, it stands to reason that a Third Temple will be rebuilt that this "man of lawlessness" defiles during a future tribulation. An alternative interpretation of 2 Thessalonians 2:4 by John Chrysostom (347-407) is that the temple refers to the Christian church as a whole.

In Revelation Chapter 11, John is told to go and measure the Temple of God. John is not likely measuring the Second Temple because most biblical scholars and early church patriarchs date the writing of Revelation around 95 AD after the destruction of the Second Temple in 70 AD. If Revelation is a vision of the future including events preceding the Day of the Lord, then the presence of a Jerusalem Temple in Revelation 11:1-2 builds the case for a Third Temple. It seems in the rest of Revelation 11 that the two witnesses are preaching from the vicinity of the Temple during their three and a half year ministry during the Tribulation.

2) A Third Temple would provide a memorial gathering place throughout the Millennial Kingdom.

Ezekiel's vision of a restored Israel with a new temple, city, and allotment of land in Ezekiel 40 to 48 has never been realized. The Second Temple built in Jerusalem after the return of the exiles from Persia, didn't fit Ezekiel's specifications. One interpretation is that Ezekiel's Temple vision was a metaphor of restored purity and vitality simply to encourage the Israelites while in Persia. We know from Rev. 21:22 that there will be no Temple in the New Jerusalem that comes after the Millennial Kingdom. "I did not see a temple in the city, because the Lord God Almighty and the Lamb are its temple."

Ezekiel's temple is a candidate for a Third Temple built and then defiled during the Tribulation. The other theory is the Ezekiel Temple is a memorial to God's faithfulness to Israel during the Millennial Kingdom.

How can a Third Temple be built when there is a Muslim mosque on the Temple Mount?

Secular liberal Jews are disgusted by the thought of a return to animal sacrifices on the Temple Mount. Since the destruction of the temple in 70 AD Judaism has, of necessity, morphed through rabbinical commentary into a system of ethical principles mixed with traditional customs. But if it is biblically consistent, Judaism has no alternative than to rebuild another Temple in Jerusalem. At that point the other requirements of the Mosaic Law (complete with the intricate Levitical priestly system, wardrobe, furnishings, red heifer cow, animal sacrifices, etc.) must be re-established. Liberal Jews are probably relieved there is a Muslim structure on the Temple site. The stalemate of temple real estate keeps liberal Judaism viable.

Even if the Orthodox Jews in Israel get their chance to reinstate a Temple based on the Torah of Moses there is still debate concerning the exact location to build. The traditional site of the first and second temples is where the Muslim Dome of the Rock now sits. Competing theories suggest alternative locations on the Temple Mount, both north and south of the Dome of the Rock, which would not require the displacement of Islam's third most sacred shrine.

The alternative site just north of the present Dome of the Rock sits near the Muslim gazebo called the Dome of the Spirit. The southern alternative site is where a fountain sits. Since the Third Temple will be a vain temple from a Christian perspective, it really doesn't have to be on the exact spot of the first two. Orthodox rabbis would completely disagree. For them the exact location is all important—down to the inch.

One scenario is that as Europe becomes more and more Islamicized, a moderate Muslim is elected with influence over a European alliance. Some moderate Muslims already support the idea of having a Jewish Temple built on the Temple Mount next to the Dome of the Rock in the name of peaceful coexistence. A moderate Muslim European leader could facilitate a deal for construction in an attempt to promote world peace.

However, if the alternative sites are not used for a Third Temple, I have four theories concerning the prospects of a semi-peaceful displacement of the gold gilded Dome of the Rock.

1) Natural Disaster - Jerusalem is in an earthquake zone. It isn't a big deal to God to shake the earth to clear the landscape if He wants to. An "act of God" could explain how the Muslim world in particular and global community in general would stand by and allow for a Third Temple building project to take place. However, since the Dome of the Rock has been built, there have been hundreds of earthquakes in Jerusalem. That is one sturdy building.

2) Terrorist Act - The Muslim world may look like one big unified community to outsiders. But the political, spiritual, cultural, and ethnic divisions in Islam are myriad. There is the strange possibility that an Islamic faction or crazed suicide bomber would blow up the Dome of the Rock in an attempt to blame Israel and incite rage for a decisive showdown that would mobilize the Muslim world to destroy the Jewish state. Or a crazed Jew or Christian may blow it up to hasten prophetic fulfillment on their own terms.

3) Human Error - During any future conflict, a stray rocket from Iran, Israel, or another country could accidentally hit the temple mount. Chaos would ensue no matter who was eventually found responsible. But the discussion of what should replace the Muslim shrine would go to another level.

4) Bargaining Chip for World Peace - The Anti-Christ Ruler himself will broker a deal for the sake of "world peace" that allows the Jews to have their most sacred House and disassemble and reconstruct Islam's third most sacred nearby. The Anti-Christ Ruler may even be a moderate Muslim with a phenomenal gift for global diplomacy. Such a deal would only be attractive if global survival were on the line in some kind of nuclear standoff between Israel and the Muslim Middle East.

Why Would God Permit Two Worship Systems to Co-exist?

There have been other seasons of transition when two paradigms of worship stood side by side in scripture and in history. Jesus' death and resurrection created One New Man out of Jew and Gentile through faith in Himself. Even as the church grew, the Jewish Temple system of worship, though obsolete, continued for nearly 40 years. The first followers of Jesus worshipped daily at the Temple Courts in Jerusalem. (Acts 2:46) God's Spirit didn't forbid them from gathering there even though they knew that Jesus could be worshipped anywhere.

There was a brief season in the time of King David when there were two centers of worship in Israel. David pitched a tent and put the Ark of the Covenant in front of singers and musicians who sang to the beauty of God out in the open. This happened while the Tabernacle of Moses was seven miles northwest of Jerusalem in Gibeon. This season that preceded the building of the first temple was unique. The open worship of night and day singing and prayer in Zion was never prescribed by the Law given to Moses. It was a transitional period when God allowed two paradigms of worship to co-exist. Many would say that the ark being set out in the open instead of behind the veil of the inner room of Moses Tabernacle is a model of the kind of New Testament worship in the church. In David's tent God accepted worship outside the boundaries of the Jewish Law. King David's worship of God in the open is a forerunner of the New Covenant worship that Jesus proclaimed to the Samaritan woman at the well:

'Sir,' the woman said, 'I can see that you are a prophet. Our fathers worshiped on this mountain, but you Jews claim that the place where we must worship is in Jerusalem.'

Jesus declared, 'Believe me, woman, a time is coming when you will worship the Father neither on this mountain nor in Jerusalem. You Samaritans worship what you do not know; we worship what we do know, for salvation is from the Jews. Yet a time is coming and has now come when the true worshipers will worship the Father in spirit and truth, for they are the kind of worshipers the Father seeks. God is spirit, and his worshipers must worship in spirit and in truth.' (John 4:19-24)

How Would a Third Temple Help Prepare Jews for the Leadership of Jesus?

While salvation is found in no one else, for there is no other name under heaven given among men by which we must be saved (Acts 4:12), I propose that a Third Jerusalem Temple could prepare rabbinical Judaism to turn to Jesus as Messiah as nothing ever has. It could happen this way. There will be euphoria in parts of the global Jewish community as the long held dream of a Third Temple in Jerusalem is erected. That honeymoon will be short-lived. The sensibilities of the modern world, including secular Judaism, will be offended by the reinstitution of animal sacrifices in an antiquated temple system. The Jewish religion will lose credibility world-wide and suffer great humiliation in the eyes of all nations.

As global anti-Semitism rises, the charismatic leader who helped create the peace treaty to resolve the Middle East impasse will realize a great leadership opportunity has arrived. By stepping in to abruptly end the Third Temple sacrifices and assuming the role of a transformational leader, he will be hailed as a savior. The economic, religious, political, educational, entertainment, cultural, and social global networks will embrace his leadership. A global consensus will form around him as this leader becomes the closest thing to a world monarch the world has ever seen. The mandate given to this man will trigger the Great Tribulation. He will be worshipped as a god because of the level of inspirational authority, influence, and power he exerts over humanity. All who resist his leadership will be marginalized to the point of persecution and death. Global insecurity and crisis will justify extreme executive powers for this Anti-Christ leader to cleanse the world of those who cling to obsolete belief systems that do not support the new world order. As a result of this power shift, many who had claimed to be followers of Jesus will change allegiances with barely a thought. This great falling away is exactly what Jesus prophecies in Matthew 24:9-13:

Then you will be handed over to be persecuted and put to death, and you will be hated by all nations because of me. At that time many will turn away from the faith and will betray and hate each other, and many false prophets will appear and deceive many people. Because of the increase of wickedness, the love of most will grow cold, but he who stands firm to the end will be saved.

Even as many jettison hope in Christ for the Anti-Christ, there will be a great harvest of those who realize that Jesus' leadership is just around the corner. This will especially be true among Jews world-wide.

While the world rejoices that it has new hope for survival and world peace, the desecration of the Third Temple and the despair it brings will cause many Jews to seriously examine the leadership of Jesus for the first time. Life for Christians and Jews in the three and a half year Anti-Christ government will be horrible. But even in the midst of the Great Tribulation, God will empower two amazing witnesses to stand near the defunct Temple in Jerusalem to preach the gospel of the Kingdom of God with unprecedented power before Jesus comes. These two preachers predicted in Revelation 11 will operate in the power of God like Moses and Elijah did in their generations. In that period many Jews will accept the leadership of Jesus. The miracles and preaching of the "Two Witnesses" will spark a Great Global Harvest among Jews and Gentiles alike.

Meanwhile, the hard labor pains of increasing global transition will intensify. The heart of the Anti-Christ and all who follow him will grow harder and harder as God pours out His Spirit on all who turn to Him and his judgment on all who oppose Him.

As the final battle between the Messiah and the world leaders who oppose Him is waged at the Jerusalem city gate (Zech 14:2-5), the stage is set to fulfill Jesus' prophecy in Matthew 23:39. The Jewish leaders of Jerusalem will say to Messiah Jesus as He comes in rescue with the angels and saints from all the ages, "Blessed is He who comes in the Name of the Lord!" This time the leaders of

Israel *will* be prepared for the leadership of Jesus. The long awaited welcome of Israel for Her Bridegroom King and Judge will be the finish line of this Age of history. Then the glorious Age of Jesus' leadership on earth begins!

Chapter 19

Looking Backward to Move Forward

"These things happened to (Israel wandering in the desert) as examples and were written down as warnings for us, on whom the fulfillment of the ages has come."
(1 Corinthians 10:11)

The Conversation Continues

Much of popular American Christianity falls within the Dispensational Premillennial camp. These brothers and sisters look forward to a future earthly reign of Jesus, along with their Historic Premillennial kin. As we discussed in chapter four, these two views disagree on the role of the Church and Israel, the priority of social ethics, and the order of events surrounding the final years of biblical End Time prophecy.

Most of the global Christian community falls within the Amillennial or Postmillennial eschatological systems. These brothers and sisters may expect some form of an earthly reign of Jesus after His return, but not in a transitional Millennial Kingdom. Whether the reign of Jesus is from Jerusalem is of little to no importance. For them the return of Christ will directly usher us into the era of the New Heavens and the New Earth. These views represent most Catholic, Orthodox, Presbyterian, Reformed, Anglican, Methodist, and other mainline protestant movements.

St. Augustine, Bishop of Hippo in Africa in the fifth century, was and is one of the most influential Christian thinkers. His articulation of the role of the Church in history in "City of God" laid a solid foundation for Amillennial and Postmillennial views for many centuries. But with the creation of an Israeli state furthering the possibility of conditions for biological Israel to be grafted back into the grace covenant of God, it is important to reexamine the Premillennial view of the first generations of Christians. Living theologians like Craig Blomberg and Walter Kaiser are voices supporting Historic Premillennialism on the academic side, while International House of Prayer - Kansas City founder, Mike Bickle, promotes Historic Premillennialism (with an emphasis on a victorious church) on the popular side.

Opponents of Premillennial views point out that the term "millennium" only appears in Revelation chapter 20. True enough. But the concept of God partnering with His Covenant People to govern the physical universe began in Genesis chapter one and is developed throughout the 66 Books. I would like to propose that parallelisms of Israel during the Exodus period illustrate a case for the progressive biblical theme of a future Millennium.

Guidance into the future is helped by gazing into the past similar to the way that an oarsman in a rowboat moves forward by facing backward. God has given clues about future redemption to those who peer into the redemptive history of the past.

Comparing Israel in the Sinai Wilderness to the World in the Millennial Kingdom

The example of Israel throughout the Old Testament is a bit like a test tube sample of a polluted lake. You don't have to test the whole lake to see what it is made of. Israel was chosen as one nation out of all the rest not because they were any better. But just in case non-Jewish peoples think they *are* any better than Israel, God is going to go ahead and test the whole lake anyway. For a thousand years.

I believe the thousand years of Jesus' Messianic leadership will demonstrate on a global scale what Israel demonstrated in the wilderness on a national scale. Even when God is present and leading through human intercessors, there will still be a process of testing to prepare the human race for the eternal state in the New Heaven and New Earth. The paradigm of a future Millennium is played out in several ways in the experience of Israel during the 40 year Exodus period:

1) A dramatic deliverance from an oppressive Pharaoh (Anti-Christ figure) in Egypt.

At the beginning of the exodus from Egypt, Israel was stunningly delivered from an Anti-Christ-like ruler in the form of Pharaoh when their backs were against the Red Sea. At the beginning of the Millennial Kingdom, Jesus will arrive out of Heaven with angel armies and all the saints to deal the decisive blow to wicked global rulers just as they think they are about to completely crush the covenant people of God on the Earth. Satan, like Pharaoh, will be cast into the Abyss in order for God to influence His People without demonic interference.

2) A continual encounter with God's presence and provision involving all five senses.

A whole Hebrew generation had the visible 24-7 presence of God over the national Prayer Room in the center of their community in the form of a pillar of smoke by day and a pillar of fire by night. All their daily bread was supernaturally provided from heaven and their clothes and shoes did not wear out for 40 years. Food and clothing was on the house! God was there in veiled form to all five senses.

A glorious city of Jerusalem will be the Messianic capital of the Earth. She will be the city of the Great King and she will shine with bright righteousness! The Millennial Age will be a Golden Era where people, land, and time enter a level of shalom and restoration under the 24-7 leadership of Jesus that will only be exceeded by the New Heaven and New Earth. The natural world will experience great restoration. Work is a gift of God and always a part of our human existence. Provision in the Millennium will come without demonic opposition and without the full resistance of the curse of Adam. Rock on!

3) A period without demonic influence when unredeemed human beings will still rebel against God's perfect leadership.

When God comes near to fallen human beings, our true human nature is revealed for what it is. Even though Israel watched God part the Red Sea for them to escape the Egyptians. Even though Israel "saw" God on Mount Sinai and heard His thundering voice. Even though God provided them with food from Heaven everyday and had His visible Presence over the Tabernacle 24/7. Even though He fought for them and cared for them and stayed in their midst continually, they resisted His leadership. Unredeemed people are natural rebels.

There is no mention of dark spiritual forces interfering with the Exodus generation except when the men of Israel go into sexual compromise with Moabite women. But before then, even Balaam's curses fell flat against the canopy of God's protective grace over Israel. The Devil could only succeed against God's People by enticing them to forfeit God's protection through sin, not through penetrating the barrier of angelic guard. Unfortunately, the result is the same.

Rev. 20:7-10 says there is a rebellion at the end of the Millennial Kingdom. Those who resist Jesus' leadership will have their chance to reject Him one last time. Could the compromise of the men of Israel who defile themselves near the end of the Exodus with Moabite women in the very camp of God foreshadow a similar compromise that God has to confront at the end of the Millennium? This is only a theory.

There are sticky questions. If the saints living in the Millennium have glorified bodies like Jesus, will they resist His leadership? If they are not resisting Him, then who is?

I do not believe that anyone with a redeemed body will be capable of sin in the Millennium. If that is the case, then there will be an unredeemed humanity that survives the Great Tribulation and comes under the leadership of Jesus. Human beings who resisted the

Anti-Christ but who did not know Jesus will enter in the Millennium. They will live long lives, but still have the ability to sin. They are those who sign up on Satan's side in the last rebellion of Revelation 20:7-10.

4) A theocratic governing priesthood is established and trained while God's people learn to accept the intercessory leadership of Moses (a type of Jesus).

The greatest accomplishment of Moses after 40 years was that he kept Israel alive through intercession. Numerous times God wanted to wipe out Israel and start over with Moses. Everyone, including Moses, was being trained and tested in the desert so that they could be a corporate light to the rest of the world.

In Exodus 19:6, God declared His desire that the whole nation of Israel represent Him as priests among all the other nations of the Earth. He would take one tribe, the tribe of Levi, as a royal priesthood in the stead of the first born son of every family of every tribe. Priests represent God to the people and the people to God. To be a priest is to be a mediator and intercessor.

The priests were the governing tribe of Israel. Their gift was not land, but proximity to God. The people rebelled against Moses, but so did some of the priests. Even Aaron and Miriam, Moses' brother and sister, resisted his leadership at one time. Moses himself had a leadership lapse when he grew frustrated with God's people and stepped out of love and into offense. God wants all His people to be citizen-priests with His heart of intercession.

God is training all of His people today to be priests with whom He can share His eternal presence. Every follower of Jesus is a priest with full unmediated access to the Throne of Grace in prayer. God not only wants individual priests, He wants a royal *nation* of priests. That is why corporate prayer gatherings are so important to enacting the will of God in the Earth even now. *Every* believer is called to intercession through personal obedience and corporate prayer. We have a thousand year training period coming up with a lot of people who survived this Age who are going to need our help to live in the next one.

In the Millennial Kingdom, God, in the form of a Moses–like mediator in Jesus, will be visibly present in our world, 24-7. Like Moses, Jesus' greatest achievement will be that He kept human beings alive throughout this current evil age through the intercession of His blood on the cross. The redeemed saints of every people group across the globe will partner with Jesus in the Millennial government just as the tribe of Levi partnered with Moses around the House of Prayer at the center of the twelve tribes of Israel in the desert and as with David when he pitched a tent for the Ark in Zion. The thousand year Jubilee priesthood will fill the Earth with the glory of constant obedience to Jesus and dialog with God's Spirit. This increase of God's government will prepare all Creation for an Eden-like future where all of redeemed humanity and creation will live with God in full face to face communion.

5) New leadership for God's prepared people to enter into the covenant promises.

Joshua and Caleb were the only elders alive to take the next generation into Canaan, the land of God's promise. The younger generation was prepared by the 40 years of testing to trust God's leadership at a level their parents never knew.

Joshua or "Y'eshua" is the same name as Jesus. Caleb was a good Hebrew, but his name literally means "dog". Dogs, like the Gentiles (non-Jews), were considered unclean. Jews would routinely refer to Gentiles as dogs. Yet Jesus, a perfect Jew, and Dog, representing a perfect Gentile, go into the Land of Promise together. I see their joint leadership as a foreshadowing of Jews and Gentiles being made into One New Man by the work of Jesus on the cross. I also see the whole of humanity being led by this redeemed One New Man of Jew and Gentile into the Millennial Leadership of Jesus. Redeemed Israel and redeemed Gentiles will function together as a global priesthood as we learn to fully and corporately trust the Leadership of God in the Person of His Son together!

Summary

God ruled Israel in the desert through Moses and the priesthood and I believe He will rule the world through Jesus and His nation of priests in the Millennium. It is a time when Satan is cast into the abyss like Pharoah and his chariot army was cast into the bottom of the sea. Like Israel in the Sinai, who complained, rebelled, and wanted to go back to Egypt, unredeemed human beings in the Millennial Kingdom will demonstrate a willful resistance to the perfect leadership of Jesus *without* Satan and his demonic influencers around. It will be a full five senses, thousand year encounter with Jesus that will prove beyond any doubt that unredeemed people are rotten to the core apart from the mercy and grace of God! However, God's glorious plan of redeeming all of humanity, creation, and time will be fully and finally vindicated as the dawn of the New Heaven and New Earth begins.

Epilogue

"Who is he who overcomes the world, but he who believes that
Jesus is the Son of God?"
(I John 5:5)

Finishing History Well

My prayer is that what I have written has caused you to love the Jesus of history, the Jesus of Heaven's Throne, and the Jesus of your heart more than before. Nothing is more important than growing an intimate relationship with Him.

I also pray that I have done a fair job of simplifying biblical terms and complicated End-Time perspectives without being simplistic. This is not an easy task given the current state of honest dissonance among God's people. I hope too that readers who do not identify themselves as followers of Jesus will feel better introduced to a family dialog spanning nearly two thousand years of church history.

Every sensitive person is feeling the mounting crisis of human history whether they look to the Bible as a source of authority or not. Current conditions are ripe for some sort of global climax in a way no generation before us has ever seen. Does the God of the Bible actually exist? Are the prophecies of Semitic writers thousands of years ago still valid for our world today? Those are the questions you may still be asking.

I have done my best to offer you a guide for understanding our urgent times using the Bible. Now, dear reader, you have my prayers as a fellow pilgrim. Ultimately, my confidence as to whether we will finish life and history well is not in you or me. My confidence is in God to reveal Himself to those who seek Him with their whole heart. God wants to be found! He has come in human history in a certain way and in a certain person who alone is worthy to be our leader.

If the Bible is truth, then the sole Leader of the future is the one born of an unwed, virgin, teenager named Mary, too poor to get a motel room on a cold night. In thirty-three years Mary's kid gave all He had to our world for the sake of loving His Father. When He returns it will be as a King more glorious than anyone can imagine, coming for a Bridal People more eager to receive Him than any generation since the first. The Holy Spirit is preparing this Bridal People from every generation all over the world to be given by the Father to His Son. Those who love the Son are His treasure! Wow. Can this really be true? Can this really be what history is all about? Love? Better than any movie? Boy meets Girl? Boy chases Girl? Boy gets Girl? God gets the girl and WE are His girl! We actually live happily ever after. No end.

Call me cheesy, but I believe this is exactly what our lives and all history is about. After all the academic searching, wars, dramas, and life perspectives, it all comes down to love—a Father's love. The grand story of the 66 books is that we are *not* alone. God is alive and He loves us more than we can ever understand. History is not pointless. At the end of life and history, Song of Solomon 7:8 is our soul's anthem back to God, "I am my beloveds and His desire is for me!" The soul that finds God finds true love and true worship. The mature Bride of Jesus Christ will finish her journey through history confident in Jesus' love for her. Embracing the journey of love with God's Son is how we finish history well. Our delight will be to follow His leadership forever!

Preparing For the Leadership of Jesus

Having watched my wife give birth to our three sons, I know that the process of childbirth is not something to look forward to in itself. However, the result of childbirth is. . . a child! The joy and excitement of beginning a new life with that new born child causes all the pain it took to bring them in to the world a passing memory.

As we consider our personal and collective futures, we might be tempted to panic and lose hope. If we don't have the soul anchor that the Lord of All wants us to have, sadly, we will do just that. But don't forget: the main message of the 66 Books is that we have so much to look forward to, in this life and in the Age that Jesus will bring when He returns!

Finishing history well isn't about barely squeaking by as a few brave survivors while looking around at the rest of the dead burning planet. Hollywood is pumping out all kinds of apocalyptic scenarios like that with the help of some TV preachers. Yes, things will get worse on a global scale before the dawn of the new Millennium. Yes, there will be a global conflict that will make previous conflicts seem like birth contractions. Yes, there will be a great betrayal and falling away of many from belief in Jesus. Sadly many will repeat the story of Judas who gave up on Jesus just before the resurrection. But no small number of people will possess the testimony of Mary of Bethany who understood her divine moment and sold everything to honor Jesus in those same last hours Judas and Mary shared with Him.

God promised father Abraham that his children would be more numerous than sands of the seashore and the stars in the heavens. I expect a great harvest of righteousness arising through brilliantly shining sons and daughters in the future. Will those who shine with radiant faces gazing on the Sun of Righteousness be a majority of the human race during the last hour? No. But that remnant won't be a small number. Just as stars shine in a dark sky, God's true saints will stand out against a dark generation. You don't look at the darkness in the clear night sky. You look at the countless shining points of light. I believe hundreds of millions of lovesick worshippers of

Jesus will burn brightly during the deepest darkness before the dawn of the Millennial Kingdom.

My prayer is that *you* are one of them!

When Elijah was having his pity party and complaining to God that he was all alone in Israel and the only voice for Yahweh against Baal, God corrected his vision and told him that "I will leave seven thousand in Israel, all the knees that have not bowed to Baal, and every mouth that has not kissed him" (1 Kings 19:18).

God has a plan to deal with the pervasive global conspiracy of modern day Baals and their human agents. His eyes are on the hearts of faithful lovers around the globe. Paul states this idea in Romans 8:18-19: "I consider that the sufferings of this present time are not worth comparing with the glory about to be revealed to us. For the creation waits with eager longing for the revealing of the children of God."

Don't give in to pity or panic. Not now. Not when we are so close to the "glory about to be revealed to us." Look up! Your Redeemer is near!

Living for the Age to come isn't about mere survival. Nor is it simply about winning souls as we punch our rapture tickets out of here before the real trouble starts. It is about pleasing God to the uttermost even as His Son did at the Cross! It is about finishing strong together as His countless Bridal People! It is about fighting for as much justice and righteousness in the Earth today as He will grant us. It is about living with more hope in the future than anyone else has a right to have. It is about the kind of life people live when they have already died to this Age to live for the Age to come.

It is time to press in to Jesus' heart with great zeal and bold love! Jesus our dear Bridegroom King and Judge is coming soon and we still have some work to do by His Spirit to make this Earth more ready for His leadership.

"The Spirit and the Bride say, 'Come!'"

I say, "Come Jesus! Please hurry! I miss you!" What do you say?

Appendices

Appendix 1

Dr. Jack L. Arnold   Equipping Pastors
Eschatological Systems   International, Inc.
                                    Cleartheology.com 2008

THE HERMENEUTICS OF PROPHECY

Hermeneutics is the Biblical science of the basic laws of the interpretation of the scripture. Hermeneutics deals with "how" a person interprets scripture not "what" he concludes. The "how", of course, will directly affect the "what" of interpretation.

GENERAL RULES OF HERMENEUTICS

Interpret Grammatically: A study of the basic meaning of a word, for a word is a vehicle of thought.

Interpret According to Context: A word study must be placed into the context of a sentence, a sentence into the context of a paragraph and a paragraph into the context of a chapter and a chapter into the context of a book. The purpose of the writing, the people addressed and the general theme of the book are all important factors to take into consideration in interpretation of scripture.

Compare Scripture with Scripture: The writing of one author should be compared with the writing of the same author in another book of scripture, and then compared with the scripture of other authors.

Interpret Unclear Passages by Clear Passages: It is best not to build a doctrine on an unclear passage; rather the clear passages should be used to throw light on the unclear passages.

THE ISSUE IN THE HERMENEUTICS OF PROPHECY

The real issue between amils and premils is over hermeneutics. How does one interpret prophecy? Does he interpret Old Testament prophecy literally or does he interpret it spiritually as all fulfilled in the church age? The question is whether one interprets the New Testament by the Old Testament or the Old Testament by the New Testament, recognizing progressive revelation (revelation in stages as that the New Testament is higher and clearer revelation than the Old Testament.).

Premils claim that they use one method of hermeneutics for the interpretation of both the Old Testament and New Testament. They use the grammatic-historical method, which is the literal method. They admit that the Bible at times has many symbols and much figurative language; yet, they claim that all symbols and figurative language connotes a literal meaning. In actuality, premils use a seemingly more literal approach to prophecy. Dispensationalists and historic premils disagree over the degree of literalness that should be used in the interpretation of prophecy.

Amils claim that the Bible is its own interpreter of prophecy and that the New Testament spiritualizes Old Testament prophecy and applies it to the church age or the gospel age. All the promises made to Israel in the Old Testament are fulfilled in the church because the church is spiritual Israel. Except in a few places such as the time, extent and nature of an earthly kingdom, postmils agree with amils in their basic interpretation.

PREMILLENNIAL HERMENEUTICS

Interpret Literally Whenever Possible: The same rule of interpretation should be used for prophecy as for all other scripture. This makes the Old Testament basic for an interpretation of the New Testament. For instance, the Old Testament speaks of a worldwide future kingdom on earth (Num. 14:21; Isa. 40:5; 49:6; Psa. 86:9; 22;27; Isa. 2:2-3), the reign of Messiah on His earthly throne (2 Sam. 7:12-16; Psa. 89:3-4, 34-36; Jer. 23:5-8; 33:20-26; Ezk. 34:23-25; 37:23-24; Mic. 4:7-8). Israel will be converted (Jer. 31:31-34; Ezk. 11:18-20, Rom. 11:26-29).

Dispensationalists and most historic premils believe that Israel will be returned to the land (Isa. 10:21-22; Ezk. 34:24,30,31; Zech. 13:9; Mal. 3:16-18). A Premil says these prophecies must find literal fulfillment or God's word and promises are weak or not kept. God's very character is at stake. These promises will find fulfillment in a yet future earthly millennium.

A premil attempts to explain most everything in his system even if some things do not fit logically into his system. It is better to stay with a literal interpretation and have some apparent contradictions then to spiritualize Old Testament scripture.

Law of Fulfillment: In the interpretation of unfulfilled prophecy, fulfilled prophecy forms the pattern. Hundreds of prophecies concerning Christ's first advent were fulfilled literally. Why not, then, a fulfillment literally of prophesies surrounding the Lord's second advent?

Amils and premils all agree that Zech. 9:9 was fulfilled literally in Christ's first advent. Amils would say that Zech. 14:16,17 must be taken figuratively and applied generally to the future blessing of the church. However, premils say this must be taken quite literally and refer to a future earthly kingdom. Amils agree that Christ is coming again (Zech. 14:1-3) but this language is figurative (Zech. 14:4,5). Can we divide a literal second coming from a literal placing of His feet on the Mount of Olives? Premils say "no!"

Give Figurative Language a Literal Meaning: The Old Testament abounds in figurative language in the area of prophecy, but all figurative or symbolic language conveys a literal truth.

Compare Prophecy with Prophecy: Each prophecy should be checked with other prophecies for all prophecy is part of God's overall plan.

Law of Time Relationship: Two future events may be so closely mingled together on the horizon of prophecy as to appear like mountains in a range of mountains, the valleys being hidden. Two prophetic events placed side by side do not necessarily have to happen simultaneously or even in immediate succession (Isa. 9:6-8; 61:1-2).

Law of Double Reference: While not all premils hold to this law (cf. J. Barton Payne, *Encyclopedia of Biblical Prophecy*, p. 121ff), it is generally held that a prophecy may have a double fulfillment, one being in the immediate circumstances and another in the distant future. There are many references in the Psalms that speak immediately of a situation particular to David but have a future fulfillment in the person of Jesus Christ (Psa. 41:9; John 13:18).

Perhaps Babylon is a good illustration of the law of double references. The rise and fall of Babylon has a near and a far view because the near view was never com pletely fulfilled (Isa. 13:19-22; Jer. 50:3a, 13 cf. Jer. 31:13 with Rev. 17:1; Jer. 51:7 with Rev. 17:4, etc.).

AMILLENNIAL HERMENEUTICS

The Old Testament Must be Interpreted by the New Testament

Augustine coined the phrase, "The Old is by the New revealed; the New is in the Old concealed." This has been an Amil hermeneutical principle since Augustine and before. An amil believes that what Christ taught by His Holy Spirit through the Apostles is final, authoritative and infallible. The key to prophecy is how the Apostle's interpreted Old Testament scripture. The Apostles do spiritualize the Old Testament and give a progressive revelation to Old Testament revelation. For example, the Old Testament speaks of a highway for preparation for the King of Israel (Isa. 40:3) and speaks of Elijah the prophet coming before the Day of the LORD (Mal. 4:5), but the New Testament says that Elijah is John the Baptist (Matt. 11:12-14; 17:16; Mark 9:11-13).

The premil answers the question of Elijah and John the Baptist by stating that John the Baptist denied he was Elijah (John 1:21) and

Luke 1:17 says that John the Baptist came in the "power and spirit" of Elijah. It is also a Jewish custom to liken one person to another if there are certain characteristics we wish to emphasize, much like we say, "He is a Daniel."

The Old Testament Is Typical and the New Testament Is the Fulfillment of the Type

The Old Testament types foreshadowed the reality of the Gospel Age in the New Testament. The whole of the Old Testament, not just the ceremonial aspects of the Mosaic Law, pointed forward to Christ and the Gospel Age (Heb. 10:1 cf.; Heb. 3:5; Col. 2:17).

1. The "seed" of the Abrahamic Covenant was Christ (Gal. 3:16).
2. Christians are spiritual seed of Christ and heirs of the Abrahamic Covenant (Gal. 3:29).
3. The church is spiritual Israel (Gal. 6:16).
4. The church is spiritually circumcised in the heart (Phil. 3:3; Rom. 2:29).
5. The tabernacle of the Old Testament. is spiritually fulfilled in the church (Acts 15: 14-18) and the church is a holy temple (Eph. 2:21-22; 1 Cor. 6:19,20).
6. Christ does sit upon His throne (Acts 2:32, 34-35) and does have a universal spiritual reign in the hearts of men (John 18:36 cf. Luke 17:21).
7. The Land of Canaan is spiritually realized in "a better country", the heavenly Jerusalem (Heb. 11:10, 16).
8. Jerusalem is really the New Jerusalem (Gal. 4:26). The real Mount Zion and the real Jerusalem are heavenly (Heb. 12:22).

The Old Covenant Has Passed Away

The Old Covenant (Mosaic economy) was temporary and everything connected with it has vanished away and is never to be restored (Heb. 8:13). The New Covenant replaces the Old Covenant; therefore, Christianity transcends, supercedes and fulfills Judaism (Gal. 3:19; Heb. 9: 6-10).

When Christ finally came, the dispensation of Law (Moses or the Old Covenant) had fulfilled its function in history. The blood of animals, feast days, the Jewish temple, Jerusalem and the "holy land" had fulfilled their functions and any return to those things now is a denial of the reality brought to us by Jesus Christ.

Divine revelation is progressive. "But the path of the just is as a shining light, that shineth more and more unto the perfect day" (Prov. 4:18). There is no going back, but always a going forward to something more glorious. There will never be a restoration of the "divers washings," "carnal ordinances" beggarly elements," and "worldly sanctuary," with its sacrifices and Levitical Priesthood, and the "middle wall of partition" between Jew and Gentile (Heb. 9:1-10; Gal. 4:9; Eph. 2:14). That has gone and gone forever; those who assert otherwise preach a revived Judaism and ancient Rabbinism and not the message of the New Testament. (G.B. Fletcher, *Predictive Prophecy,* "Seven Principles of Interpretation")

The Symbolic Must Be Interpreted by the Didactic

We should not try to build a theory on passages that are written in a symbolical context. Doctrinal positions, even in prophecy must be by straightforward teaching (didactic) passages. For instance, many passages on the second coming of Christ are not clear, but a very clear passage is 2 Peter 3:1-14. The context is about the second advent of Christ and there is a chronological time sequence: Christ will come suddenly and unexpectedly (v. 10), the present earth will be destroyed by fire (vs. 10, 12) and then will come the "new heavens and new earth" or the eternal state (v. 13).

CONCLUSION

It seems as though a safe basic principle in the hermeneutics of prophecy would be: *take every passage literally unless there is some compelling reason to take it otherwise.* This compelling reason will normally be a plain didactic passage in the New Testament.

We should keep control over our hermeneutical system by letting the literal control the typological. Therefore, we should interpret prophecy literally unless the implicit or explicit teaching of the New Testament suggests typological (spiritual) interpretation.

Appendix 2

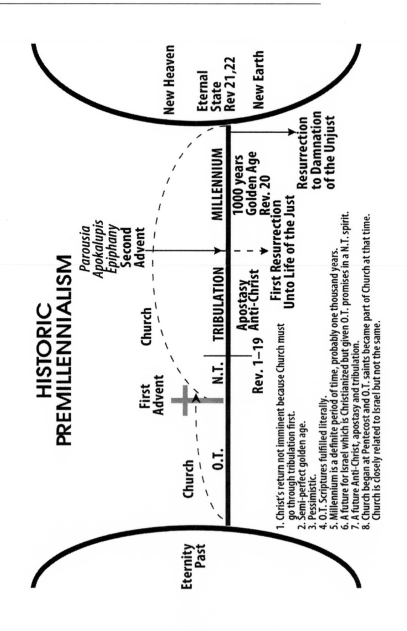

HISTORIC PREMILLENNIALISM

Eternity Past

Church

O.T.

First Advent

Church

N.T.

Parousia
Apokalupis
Epiphany
Second Advent

TRIBULATION
Rev. 1–19

Apostasy
Anti-Christ

MILLENNIUM

1000 years
Golden Age
Rev. 20

First Resurrection
Unto Life of the Just

Resurrection
to Damnation
of the Unjust

New Heaven

Eternal
State
Rev 21,22

New Earth

1. Christ's return not imminent because Church must go through tribulation first.
2. Semi-perfect golden age.
3. Pessimistic.
4. O.T. Scriptures fulfilled literally.
5. Millennium is a definite period of time, probably one thousand years.
6. A future for Israel which is Christianized but given O.T. promises in a N.T. spirit.
7. A future Anti-Christ, apostasy and tribulation.
8. Church began at Pentecost and O.T. saints became part of Church at that time. Church is closely related to Israel but not the same.

Appendix 3

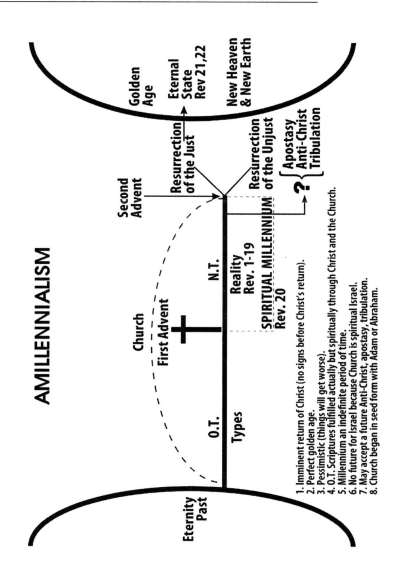

AMILLENNIALISM

Eternity Past

O.T. — Types

Church — First Advent

N.T.

Reality Rev. 1-19

SPIRITUAL MILLENNIUM Rev. 20

Second Advent

Resurrection of the Just

Resurrection of the Unjust

Apostasy
Anti-Christ
Tribulation

Golden Age

Eternal State Rev 21,22

New Heaven & New Earth

1. Imminent return of Christ (no signs before Christ's return).
2. Perfect golden age.
3. Pessimistic (things will get worse).
4. O.T. Scriptures fulfilled actually but spiritually through Christ and the Church.
5. Millennium an indefinite period of time.
6. No future for Israel because Church is spiritual Israel.
7. May accept a future Anti-Christ, apostasy, tribulation.
8. Church began in seed form with Adam or Abraham.

Appendix 4

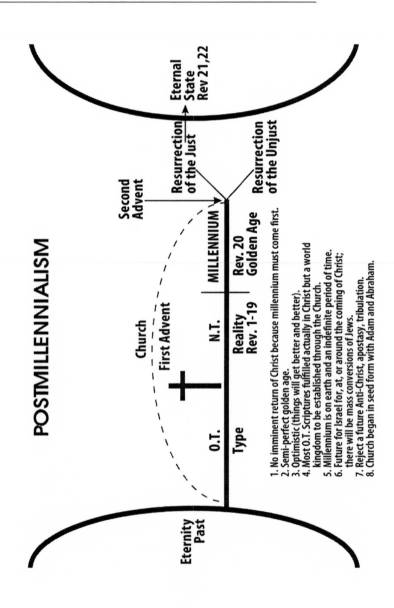

POSTMILLENNIALISM

Eternity Past

Church
First Advent

O.T. — N.T. — MILLENNIUM

Second Advent

Resurrection of the Just

Resurrection of the Unjust

Eternal State
Rev 21,22

Type — **Reality Rev. 1-19** — **Rev. 20 Golden Age**

1. No imminent return of Christ because millennium must come first.
2. Semi-perfect golden age.
3. Optimistic (things will get better and better).
4. Most O.T. Scriptures fulfilled actually in Christ but a world kingdom to be established through the Church.
5. Millennium is on earth and an indefinite period of time.
6. Future for Israel for, at, or around the coming of Christ; there will be mass conversions of Jews.
7. Reject a future Anti-Christ, apostasy, tribulation.
8. Church began in seed form with Adam and Abraham.

Appendix 5

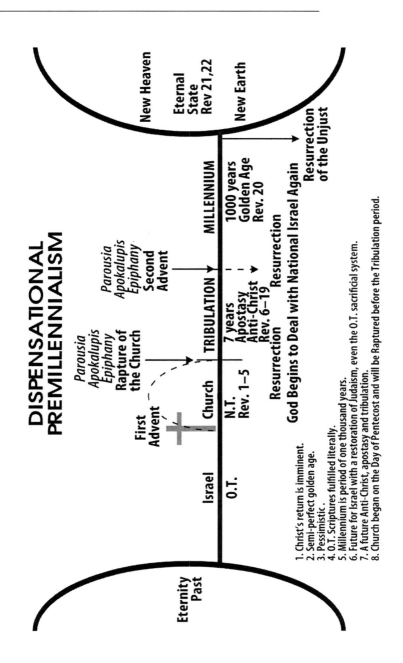

DISPENSATIONAL PREMILLENNIALISM

Eternity Past

Israel — O.T.

First Advent
Parousia Apokalupis Epiphany
Rapture of the Church

Church — N.T. Rev. 1–5

Resurrection

TRIBULATION — 7 years Apostasy Anti-Christ Rev. 6–19

Parousia Apokalupis Epiphany
Second Advent

Resurrection

God Begins to Deal with National Israel Again

MILLENNIUM — 1000 years Golden Age Rev. 20

Resurrection of the Unjust

New Heaven

Eternal State Rev 21,22

New Earth

1. Christ's return is imminent.
2. Semi-perfect golden age.
3. Pessimistic.
4. O.T. Scriptures fulfilled literally.
5. Millennium is period of one thousand years.
6. Future for Israel with a restoration of Judaism, even the O.T. sacrificial system.
7. A future Anti-Christ, apostasy and tribulation.
8. Church began on the Day of Pentecost and will be Raptured before the Tribulation period.

Appendix 6

Interpreting the Book of Revelation

Much of the information in this appendix is taken from T. L. Frazier's, *A Second Look at the Second Coming*.

Literary Styles and Personal Encounters

The Revelation given to John, the 66th Book of the Bible, has presented the greatest number of challenges for biblical interpreters over the centuries. This is partly because it is written in a genre of Jewish and then Christian literary style popular from 200 BC to 200 AD called "apocalyptic". Apocalypse means "uncovering" or "unveiling". Apocalyptic literature is characterized by angelic messengers who give divine disclosures to human agents concerning human events. Apocalyptic writings were filled with strong messianic expectations for a heavenly deliverance of the oppressed people of God. The apocalyptic writing style with its symbolic imagery makes it easy to simply view the book of Revelation as a mystical first century riddle. But while apocalyptic writers were addressing the history of their day in symbolic terms, when properly understood, those images can have meaning now.

The book of Revelation is not exclusively apocalyptic in style. It is also written by John as a prophecy using the prophetic literary style as well. Apocalyptic was not concerned with social change as much as it described the confrontation between good and evil forces. Prophetic writing is concerned about immediate transformation. Revelation chapters 2 and 3 are letters to seven churches in Asia Minor with prophetic warnings and blessings offered pending the immediate response of those communities to the leadership of Jesus. The Revelation to John carries both ultimate *and* immediate visions and messages.

The imagery that John reports seeing in Heaven is similar to the prophetic visions of Daniel and Ezekiel and even of the vision of God on Mount Sinai in Exodus 24:9 recorded by Moses. I believe it is a mistake to view the language of apocalyptic and prophetic writings as mere genres. I believe what is written by these men was born of genuine personal encounters with the real and living God. Heaven is a real place. The Throne Room of God is a real place. If anything, *this* world is less "real" than the world we cannot see yet. I believe we are reading descriptions of things these men really saw with spiritual eyes.

Since everything in heaven and earth belongs to the Lord who made it, He is about reclaiming all that is His. He affirms this world and our history, but from His perspective. That is what we need most in any hour. God's perspective! So no matter what the circumstances of a generation, the Throne Room perspective is the one needed most. That is what the book of Revelation gives us. That is why, in the grace of God, similar biblical spiritual encounters are the inheritance of any follower of Jesus at any time.

Date of Authorship

John's revelation was written during a time of persecution in the church. The early church fathers, including Irenaus of Lyons (AD 120-190), Clement of Alexandria (AD 150-215), and Jerome (AD 342-420) asserted that the Apostle John authored the Revelation on the island of Patmos during the AD 91 to 96 persecution by the Roman Emperor Domitian. Though not supported by early church tradition, some Bible interpreters today argue for an early date of authorship during the AD 64 to 68 persecution of the Roman Christians under Emperor Nero.

Audience and Message

Beyond its application to the original audience of John's day, the message of the Revelation has encouraged followers of Jesus for 2000 years. The vision of the ultimate salvation of God's people through Jesus' triumph over all opposing forces in creation has been powerfully motivating to every generation. Jewish apocalyptic literature, though symbolic in its language, is actually focused on real human history. The power of the visions written by Daniel, Ezekiel, and John, are that they root the reality of this world in the greater reality of a heavenly unseen world where a very good and powerful God is in full ultimate control. Hallelujah indeed!

It is no wonder then, that different methods for interpreting the last book of the Bible have been developed.

Methods of Interpreting Revelation

Preterism - "Preterism" comes from Latin meaning "past". This method interprets Revelation entirely through the lens of the first century context in which it was written. This approach is popular among biblical scholars because there are strong correlations between the historical context at the writing of Revelation (especially if written before the Temple was destroyed in AD 70) and the historical events as recorded by Flavius Josephus (AD 37 – 100), a Jewish soldier/historian, who witnessed the Roman-Jewish War (AD 66-70).

Futurism - Futurism acknowledges that John was writing to the church of the first century, but also believes Revelation is a blueprint prophecy for the generation that will experience the events surrounding the return of Jesus. This view is popular because it grants permission for readers to interpret Revelation in the context of the daily news. Unchecked, this method can produce wild and sometimes dangerous interpretations. More than one author and TV preacher has gotten rich producing fantastic End Time scenarios for a curious public.

Historicism - This view was first developed by Joachim of Flora (1132-1202) an Italian monk of the medieval period. This view became popular during the Protestant Reformation and applies the prophecies of Revelation to the historical events that mainly focused on Western Europe. The weakness of this view is that it is not relevant to the audiences of the first century or today.

Idealism – This interpretive method sees few references to actual history, past, present, or future. Revelation's message is seen as spiritual truth relevant to all Christians at all times. The problem is that it separates John's symbols from the historical settings and spiritual encounters he probably had in mind. Apocalyptic writing may be poetic, but its symbols point to concrete realities.

Combining the Methods

In our post-modern culture where multiple paradigms are encouraged, it is easier to blend interpretive methods. This approach may be more right than wrong, if done in the light of the whole 66 Books, I believe it is simply wise and straightforward to accept that all of the above approaches are valid in their own way to a certain degree. In fact, combining all four views provides the kind of interpretive checks and balances that are often needed where understanding Revelation is concerned.

God is unchanging in His nature and transcendent over all creation. Yet He has chosen to reveal Himself over time through real people in an imminent and personal way. Therefore, the task of biblical interpretation naturally involves a constant reaffirmation and application of the ancient text in the light of current events. This does not necessarily strip earlier generations of what was the proper revelation they gained for their day. It means that the eternal truth of God transcends human history and is always relevant in some dynamic way to anyone reading or hearing His Word.

ESCHATOLOGICAL SYSTEMS

Glossary of Terms

- **Allegorical Interpretation**: A going behind the plain meaning of scripture to the deeper spiritual meaning.
- **Amillennial**: A word that means "no one thousand." This is a theory that states that the millennium is real but spiritual and refers to the period of time between the first and second advents of Christ. This period either refers to the reign of martyred saints in heaven or saints on earth in the inter-advent period.
- **Antichrist**: A yet future character that will come to power in the tribulation before the Lord returns.
- **Apocalyptic**: Biblical prophetic language that is basically figurative and symbolical.
- **Church**: The "called out ones."
- **Covenants**: The promises God made to Israel in the Old Testament: Abrahamic, Palestinian, Davidic, Mosaic and New Covenants.
- **Didactic**: A teaching passage of scripture not filled with figurative language.
- **Dispensationalism**: This is a theory that makes a sharp distinction between Israel and the church. The outcome is a premillennialism that sees the second advent of Christ occurring in two stages either (one for the church and one for Israel) before or in the middle of the tribulation period.
- **Eschatology**: A study of last things.
- **Finalism**: This is another word used of amils. This view states that all of the prophecies of the Old Testament will end with the second advent.

- **Great Tribulation**: A period, probably 3 ½ years, of tribulation before the second advent.
- **Hermeneutics**: The laws for the interpretation of scripture.
- **Historic Premillennial**: A type of premillennialism that sees the church going through the tribulation and will be raptured just before (or at the same time) the second advent of Jesus Christ. This view also acknowledges the church to be spiritual Israel and stresses the similarities between Israel and the church.
- **Imminency**: Christ can return at any moment without any signs being fulfilled.
- **Kingdom**: The rule of Christ whether spiritual or earthly.
- **Millennium**: A Latin word meaning one thousand. Theologically it refers to a yet future golden age.
- **Midtribulational Rapture**: The church will be caught up in the middle of the seven year Tribulation.
- **Partial Rapture**: Only the spiritual Christians in the church will be caught up, and the rest of the unspiritual Christians will be left to go through the Tribulation.
- **Premillennial**: A word that actually means "before one thousand." This is a theory that states that Christ will return in His second advent and establish an earthly kingdom for one thousand literal years.
- **Presuppositions**: Basic underlying facts or assumptions behind a given thought or concept.
- **Pretribulational Rapture**: The church will be caught up before the Tribulation; therefore, it escapes the sufferings on the Tribulation period.
- **Postmillennial**: A word meaning "after one thousand." This is a theory that states that the millennium will occur on earth and then Christ will return.
- **Posttribulational Rapture**: The church will be caught up at the end of the Tribulation at the time of the second advent.
- **Progressive Dispensationalism**: A relatively new type of dispensationalism that sees a much closer relationship between the Old and New Testaments. Therefore, there is not a clear distinction between Israel and the church. They even call the church spiritual Israel. Yet, they are still pretribulational and premillennial.

- **Rapture**: A Latin word that means, "to be caught up." Biblically this refers to what will happen to the church at the coming of Christ and the Tribulation.
- **Realized Millennialism**: This is an amil concept, which states that the millennium is already realized in the gospel age.
- **Second Advent**: Christ will return to this earth literally and bodily.
- **Spiritualization**: A giving up of a literal interpretation for a spiritual interpretation of scripture.
- **Tribulation**: A yet future period of unprecedented trouble for the world that will end at the second advent of Christ.
- **Unrealized Millennialism**: The millennium has not yet been actually realized in history.

Works Cited

Arnold, Dr. Jack L., Eschatological Systems. Cleartheology.com. 2008

Dickens, Mark. Nestorian Christianity in Central Asia. 2001.

Ellul, Jacques. Money and Power. Downers Grove, IL: Intervarsity Press, 1984.

Eshleman, Paul. Call2All.org, Church Presence Among Unengaged People Groups http://call2all.org/Groups/1000014484/Call2All/Themes/UUPGs/UUPGs.aspx

Frazier, T. L. A Second Look at the Second Coming. Ben Lomond, CA: Conciliar Press, 1999.

Gruber, Dan. The Church and the Jew: The Biblical Relationship.

Hanover, NH: Elijah Publishing, 2001.

Ladd, George Eldon. The Blessed Hope. Grand Rapids, MI: Eerdman's, 1956.

Pawson, David. When Jesus Returns. London: Hodder & Stoughton, 1995.

Tolkien, J. R. R. The Letters of J. R. R. Tolkien. Ed. Humphrey

Carpenter. New York: Houghton Mifflin, 1981.

Further Reading

Ateek, Naim. Justice and Only Justice. Maryknoll, NY: Orbis Books, 1989

Bickle, Mike. Mikebickle.org Online Teaching Library

Blomberg, Craig L., and Sung Wook Chung, eds. A Case for Historic Premillennialism. Grand Rapids, MI: Baker Academic, 2009.

Bock, Darrell, ed. Three Views on the Millennium and Beyond. Grand Rapids, MI: Zondervan, 1999.

Clouse, Robert G, ed. The Meaning of the Millennium. Downers Grove, IL: Intervarsity Press, 1977.

Dolphin, Lambert, ed. "Preparations for a Third Jewish Temple." Moving Towards a Third Temple. 14 March 2009. <http://www. templemount.org/tempprep.html>.

Dowley, Tim, ed. Eerdman's Handbook to the History of Christianity. Carmel, NY: Lion Publishing, 1977.

Greig, Pete and David Roberts. Red Moon Rising. Lake Mary, FL Relevant Media, 2003

Grudem, Wayne. The Gift of Prophecy in the New Testament and Today. Westchester, IL: Crossway Books, 1988.

Hattaway, Paul, et al. <u>Back to Jerusalem</u>. Atlanta, GA: Piquant, 2003.

Humphreys, Billy. <u>Until He Comes</u>. Kansas City, MO: Forerunner Publishing, 2009

Intrater, Keith, and Dan Juster. <u>Israel, The Church, and The Last Days</u>. Shippensburg, PA: Destiny Image Publishers, 2003.

Oden, Thomas, and William Weinrich, ed. <u>Ancient Christian Commentary on Scripture, New Testament XII, Revelation</u>, Downers Grove, IL InterVarsity Press, 2005

Pate, Marvin, ed. <u>Four Views on the Book of Revelation</u>. Grand Rapids, MI: Zondervan, 1998.

Richardson, Joel. <u>Anti-Christ: Islam's Awaited Messiah</u>. Enumclaw, WA: Pleasant Word, 2006.

Ryrie, Charles C. <u>Dispensationalism Today</u>. Chicago: Moody Press, 1965.

Schaeffer, Francis A. <u>The God Who is There</u>. Downers Grove, IL InterVarsity Press 1998

Sizer, Stephen. <u>Christian Zionism</u>. Leicester, England: Intervarsity Press, 2004.

Thielman, Frank. <u>Theology of the New Testament</u>. Grand Rapids: Zondervan, 2005.

Ministry Information

Paul Hughes is President of Kingdom Forerunners. Kingdom Forerunners was founded June 1, 2007 in Birmingham, Alabama as a Christian prayer leadership ministry.

paul@kingdomforerunners.com

The Purpose of Kingdom Forerunners is to prepare our generation for the leadership of Jesus by calling us to watch and pray, work for justice, and preach God's Kingdom. Kingdom Forerunners oversees numerous ministries including the Birmingham Prayer Furnace, Campus Prayer Networks, and Redigging the Wells.

Kingdomforerunners.com.

The Birmingham Prayer Furnace is a night and day, city-wide, house of prayer and worship that contends for the city of Jesus' dreams. Like the 24/7 iron blast furnaces in the Steel City of old, the Birmingham Prayer Furnace seeks for the fiery love of the Father to be poured in to the hearts of His children. Night and day, corporate worship and prayer fuels intimacy with Jesus, involvement in His mission, and calls the Bride of Christ in Metro Birmingham, Alabama to live with integrity and urgency until her Bridegroom King and Judge returns.

Birminghamprayerfurnace.com.

Redigging The Wells is a prayer movement for releasing justice in Jesus name to a new generation. Regional spiritual transformation involves healing generational wounds and renewing generational covenants to move cultures forward with biblical Kingdom values under the leadership of Jesus. Unified, corporate prayer at key places, with key people, at key times bring reconciliation, redemption, and transformation.

Rediggingthewells.org

Kingdom Forerunners Values

These biblical values undergird all of the ministries of Kingdom Forerunners.

1) Abiding in the Love of the Father

Abiding in the love of the Father is paramount to loving Jesus, loving the leadership of His Holy Spirit, loving His Word, loving His community, loving His mercy and justice, and loving His global Purpose.

2) Relationships and Healthy Community Rhythm Before Vision

We trust God to expand His work through a growing network of deepening friendships. We desire a stable core community that sustains healthy long term rhythms of work, worship, and rest. Corporate vision grows out of corporate Christ centered prayer, not a one man show.

3) Character Before Gifts

God values character, competence, and charisma, but growing Christ-like character shown by the fruit of the Spirit comes first.

4) Urgency of the Hour

The biblical signs of the times require our serious commitment to living as a generation prepared to see the return of the Lord. Understanding our climactic season in history is critical to the way we live

5) Openness to the Voice, Supernatural Gifts, and Leadership of the Holy Spirit

Jesus sent us the Holy Spirit to lead, teach, and empower us and He is quite able to do so. The Bride of Christ will increasingly radiate with trust in the leadership of Jesus as she walks in step with His Spirit during increasing global pressure.

6) Unity of the Sprit in the One Bride of Christ

Competition, jealousy, political maneuvering, gossip, and slander are from the dark side. The Bride of Christ transcends organizational, economic, ethnic, and cultural lines in any region. We must contend for the unity that Jesus purchased for us on the cross and learn to consider others better than ourselves through mutual submission.

7) Developing Prayer Friendly Cultures

The activity of group prayer involves the incorporation of various styles, philosophies, theologies, and practices that often conflict at a cultural and practical level. Leaders of corporate prayer gatherings need to become masters of discernment and cultural diplomacy in order to preserve the power of prayer across a city through agreement at the deepest heart level.

8) Counter-cultural Lifestyles of Simplicity, Gentleness, and Conviction

We cannot warn our generation if we live their worldly values system. The Sermon on the Mount culture and our willing response to live counter-cultural lifestyles now for a soon coming Kingdom is a privilege. Kingdom lifestyles go beyond personal piety and national politics to loving enemies and counting it joy to suffer for a gentle King of Kings who will one day crush all the other kings of the earth who oppose His leadership.

9) Multi-ethnic Ministry and Racial Justice

Birmingham as a city and Alabama as a state have a redemptive gift for releasing racial healing and justice to the earth. God has invited the Body of Christ in this area to walk out the dream of "Beloved Community" birthed in the Church of the Deep South in the 1950's for the sake of the healing of the Nations. The leadership core must understand and reflect this conviction.

Become a Ministry Partner of Kingdom Forerunners

The ministries of Kingdom Forerunners touch many lives through cultivating a Sermon on the Mount lifestyle of watching and praying, working for justice, and preaching God's Kingdom. Become a Kingdom Forerunner by joining the email list of one of the KF ministries. Donate to help build 24/7 prayer in Birmingham, grow movements of regional transformation, or fuel campus prayer networks. Participate in the prayer rooms, conferences, and ministry intensives that develop each year.

Order More Copies of The Finishing Well Series

Books in the Finishing Well Series may be ordered though any bookstore, through amazon.com, barnesandnoble.com, google.com, xulonpress.com, or kingdomforerunners.com. These books are also available as ebooks. All proceeds from sales go into the nonprofit ministries of Kingdom Forerunners. If benefitting Kingdom Forerunners is important to you, ordering printed books from kingdomforerunners.com generates the most support. Thank you!

CPSIA information can be obtained at www.ICGtesting.com
Printed in the USA
BVOW070005160812

297911BV00001B/11/P